D0170691

Hip-Hop

vs.

MAAT:

A Psycho/Social Analysis of Values

by Jawanza Kunjufu

African American Images
Chicago, Illinois

Cover design by Fred Anderson

Cover illustration by Reginald Mackey

Photo credits: George Harris

First edition, first printing

Copyright 1993 by Jawanza Kunjufu

Acknowledgments

To my Lord and Savior, Jesus Christ, our editorial staff, Doriel Mackay and Kimberly Vann. To my wife, Rita, who is both my partner in business and a true "help meet", and my sons, Walker and Shikamana, who continue to inspire me and demonstrate the importance of values.

To my supporters, to whom I shall always be grateful. For without your input (both praises and criticisms), I could not grow.

Dedication Request

Please pass a copy of this book to a member of the
Hip-Hop, New Jack generation.

Table Of Contents

Introduction I

Chapter One
Values 1

Chapter Two
Satan's Agenda 40

Chapter Three
When and How Values Are Taught 75

Chapter Four
From Nehemiah to Clarence 113

Conclusion 130

References 147

Hip-Hop

vs.

MAAT:

A Psycho/Social Analysis of Values

INTRODUCTION

This is the twelfth book that I've written beginning in 1982 with my best seller *Countering the Conspiracy to Destroy Black Boys.* I remember Smokey Robinson who has been singing for over 35 years mentioning that he never knows if his record is going to be a success. Records that he thought should have been hits weren't and songs that he had some doubts about became best sellers. The same thing applies to me. As a writer, I have noticed that books which are controversial and possess numerous polemic statements unfortunately seem to sell better than books that many times are well written, have issues that are qualified, well-researched, and presented objectively.

I've observed on talk shows that when I'm interviewed about the conspiracy to destroy black boys there is an unlimited number of callers, but when we talk about *Developing Positive Self-Images* or *Motivating Black Youth to Work,* the callers are fewer. I've also observed that the callers about the first book love to talk about the plight of Black males and the awesomeness of White male supremacy. I've even noticed that when we mention that the book is actually ''countering'' which means there are solutions to these problems along with ''developing'' and ''motivating'' that many people are less interested in discussing solutions versus the problem.

I've always felt that *Motivating and Preparing Black Youth to Work* was a better book than *Countering the Conspiracy to Destroy Black Boys.* While *Motivating and Preparing Black Youth to Work* has sold well, it has not nearly sold as well as the million copies of *Countering the Conspiracy to Destroy Black Boys.* I wanted to preface *Hip Hop vs. MAAT: A Psycho/Social Analysis of Values* with these comments because I now believe

I

that this is the best book that I've ever written. It took me a long time to finally write this book because values affect everything we do and yet it is so hard to determine when they are taught and who taught them. For that reason it becomes even more difficult to change values that are not Africentric, especially if a person has now become a young adult or older.

Let me first define the four major values and characters that we'll be looking at throughout the book. The first one is "Hip-Hop" which can be defined as: music centered, rebellious, the assertive voice of urban youth and is shaped by the language, culture, fashions, hairstyles, and world view of a generation alienated not only from the Eurocentric dominant culture but to a surprising degree from its African American heritage. Hip-Hop is in many respects a classic youth oppositional subculture rejecting the norms and values of the mainstream, measuring success in terms of peer approval and equating power with the ability to influence the subculture constantly changing insider cues, taste and values. Its strengths are its energy and creativity.

Hip-Hop is a term derived from an early New York rapper named "Lovebug Starski." He coined it in the phrase "chap hippity hop don't stop keep on body rock". The term was then popularized by Afrika Bambaataa who is the leader of a nonviolent organization called the Zulu Nation. Hip-Hop is a highly dynamic culture whose very nature is change. This dynamism has even been captured in the term "the flava" short for "flavor of the month". This implies that trends are cycled monthly. The street life of a message refers to the time it has in "value" or is viewed as part of the culture. Messages typically have a very limited street life. As soon as adults become aware of the terminology, Hip-Hop feels the need to move on to another flava.

II

The second value and character that we want to look at throughout the book will be New Jack , the term defined and popularized in the movie *New Jack City*. New Jack refers to the voice of a new generation of youth. Its popularity revolves around the new attitudes, behaviors and creative terminology of African American youth. This male-centered culture feels the need to show disregard for personal safety as a sign of membership. At-risk behavior could take on a variety of forms including substance abuse, promiscuity, academic failure, being a street player, and/or other characteristics. New Jacks demand an uncritical adherence to its orthodoxies as a condition of acceptance. The need for acceptance from peers seems to be more influential than even the need for personal safety. In fact, we found that on an individual level, the degree of knowledge in addition to attitudes regarding at-risk behavior were impressive. To be a member of such a society, exile is a prospect less dreadful than death itself. An outcast, at least in his or her own perception, has no other community to join.[1] Our challenge throughout the book is to move those people that demonstrate the values of Hip-Hop and New Jack to the following values of MAAT and the Nguzo Saba.

MAAT is expressed in the seven cardinal virtues of righteousness, truth, justice, harmony, balance, reciprocity, and order. MAAT is the right way, or path of righteousness. In addition to being the right and true way early in the old Egyptian kingdom (2750 through 2180 B.C.E.), MAAT acquired the sense of being the cosmic, natural and social order established by Ra, God at the time of creation. MAAT is not only the right order but also the object of human activity. MAAT is both the task which man sets for himself and also as righteousness, the promise and reward which await him on fulfilling it. It is in recognition and pursuit of this that moral ecology of shared commitments in the cognitive and affective sense are established and sustained.

III

MAAT is the basis for the ontological unity between God and humans. Ptah-Hotep's urging was to strive for excellence in all you do.[2] The other value system that we want to talk about in addition to Hip-Hop and New Jack is the Nguzo Saba defined as: Umoja - unity, Kujichagulia - self-determination, Ujima - collective work and responsibility, Ujamaa - cooperative economics, Nia - purpose, Kuumba - creativity, and Imani - faith. These are the seven principles and days of Kwanzaa which come from the African philosophical frame work called Kawaida developed by Maulana Karenga.

It is our objective throughout this book to better understand the individuals that possess a Hip-Hop and New Jack value system and attempt to move them toward MAAT and the Nguzo Saba. This will be attempted through five chapters. The first one is a collection of short stories trying to make values which often times are the "invisible institution" come to life and more concrete. The second chapter is a look at external forces, the power of the media, and the relationship between advertising and value development. The third chapter observes when and how values are developed and whether negative values can be changed. The fourth chapter looks at the role that values play in empowering our community and how people like Clarence Thomas is not an anomaly. He is the embodiment of the American value system. Clarence represents an older version of New Jack. The final chapter, the conclusion, analyzes some of the pertinent issues where values are being discussed on a regular basis: marriage, divorce, abortion, drugs, gun control, etc. Let's now experience how values are portrayed each and every day in our lives.

IV

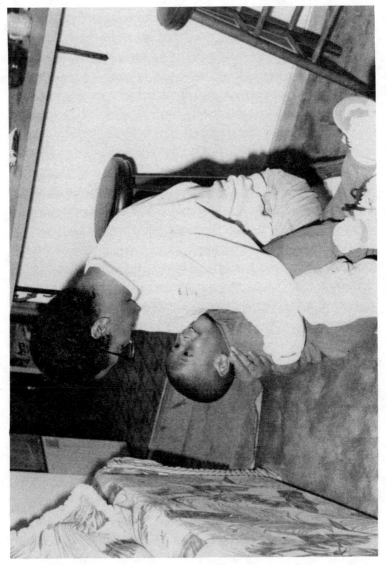

Parents must reclaim the responsibility of being their child's first teacher.

CHAPTER ONE

Values

"We're creating a society where cheaters prosper and you can't honestly tell children that honesty is the best policy"
---Ralph Wexler, Institute of Ethics

Values/Work Ethic

"Mama, did Pat get off to school on time?", Ramona asked her mother. She didn't know what time it was. It was a hot, lazy afternoon and she had been up pretty late last night. She was wondering if her little girl had gotten off to school on time. The clock said 1:45 p.m. It was almost time for little Patricia to be returning home. Ramona was having a very difficult time getting out of bed. She laid there wondering and watching her life go by in panoramic color. She remembered how excited she was about going to school and then she reflected when school became boring.

She fell in love with Keith and had a daughter, Patricia. Her mother said that she didn't want the same thing happening to Ramona that happened to her. She had a baby before her fifteenth birthday, but Ramona didn't listen. She smiled and said, "I did listen. I listened to Keith's rap and here I am, just me, Patricia and this measly welfare check. Maybe tomorrow I'll go out and look for a job if I wake up on time. Or maybe I'll try to find Keith." Ramona laughs and thinks to herself, "I don't know which one would be more

1

difficult, finding me a job or finding my man." She rolls back over and waits to hear Patricia knock on the door returning home from school.

———

Across town, Sue and Jane are sitting at the coffee table. They are two of the 300,000 White female widows who also don't work. They marvel at the flowers Jane has planted in the backyard and Sue asks when can Jane come by her house and share her green thumb in her garden. As they stroll into the den to watch their favorite soap opera, Jane responds, "I've been pretty busy for the past few days, but I'm sure that maybe next week I'll be able to get by."

———

Darryl and Claude were sitting on a bench in the park. They both had been laid off from work for the past eighteen months. Darryl got laid off from U.S. Steel and Claude used to work at GM in Flint until the plant moved to a small town in Mexico. Claude said, "Man, we were making some good money, eighteen dollars an hour, benefits, and five weeks of vacation. I just can't get my old lady to understand that I'm not working no minimum wage job. She can go type letters if she wants to. She can ring up the sales at JC Penney if she wants to. I don't care if she gets on her knees and cleans up the "master's house", but I'm not working no minimum wage job." Darryl nods while Claude is talking and says, "I understand man, but you know it's hard when you see your woman going off to work and you see your little boy and girl look in your eyes and ask for a pair of gym shoes and when you say you don't

2

have any money they ask why don't you go to work like mama. I can tell my old lady that I'm not working for minimum wage, but I tell you Claude, I don't know how to explain that to my children.'' Claude agrees and passes the wine bottle to Darryl.

Values/Life

Nobody knew but Renee as she drove her mother's car late in the evening toward the beach. Her boyfriend nor her mother knew that she was two months pregnant. As she walked along the beach, she wondered what to do - abortion or adoption. She giggled to herself and spelled the words because they were so close and yet they were light years apart. ''I'm glad my mama didn't abort me,'' she thought. She pondered whether she could carry this baby for nine months and then give it to somebody else.

Renee continued to walk along the beach and then giggled some more while thinking, ''I could just walk into the water and end it all.'' She quickly reconsidered and said, ''It ain't that serious.'' As she walked through the sand, it felt moist to her feet. She tried to imagine what her mother would say. She would be disappointed in her little girl getting pregnant before graduation. Renee giggled again because she knew after her mother put her on five years punishment she would help raise the child. Then she thought about her boyfriend Kevin. As fine as he was, a good dancer and a hell of an athlete, she knew Kevin wasn't ready to be a daddy. Kevin was having his own problems trying to get out of 10th grade.

She thought more about adoption and wondered if she would have visitation privileges. She made a note to herself that she'd have to look into that with the Department of Human Services tomorrow. As she continued her journey along the beach, the walk became more difficult. Renee had gotten away from the house, her mother and Kevin, but she was really trying to get away from God because she knew what He wanted her to do. She was anxiously hoping that walking along the beach would allow her to find out what she wanted to do. She painfully realized that even on the beach, the Lord was there waiting for her decision.

Values/Money

On one edition of Geraldo, the life of prostitution was examined. Two prostitutes were sitting on the stage. Both of the women were married and had children. They described in their own personal way why they made the decision that they did. They commented that it was simply a job. One of the married prostitutes had her husband sitting next to her. One sounded more like an economist as she delineated step by step how the economy is in trouble, unemployment is rampant and wages are down while the cost of living spirals.

Another one shared with the audience that she used to make $34,000 a year before her erstwhile employer began a massive layoff. She asked the audience, "Where am I going to make that kind of money in this depressed economy?" Geraldo then asked, "Can you describe a particular night?" One of the prostitutes replied and said, "It's all very nice. The businessmen call me early in the afternoon at my call girl agency that I own. Sometimes all they want is dinner. That costs between $300 and $350. Others want dinner and a show and that will cost $700, and for the entire evening, and I think you know Geraldo what I mean by entire, if they want the entire evening that will be $1,200." The audience gasped in amazement at the figures that were shared. She crossed her legs, looked at the audience and said, "Now where else can I make $1,200 a night?"

4

Geraldo then asked the husband of another prostitute, "How can you be married to someone knowing that's how she's spending her evenings?" He replied, "It's hard, and we're having problems right now." His wife smirked and said, "But you know the things that we want and you know this is the way for us to secure them."

In a clip from the film, *Up Against the Wall* there's a dialogue between two brothers, Sean, the young student and his older brother Jesse, the drug dealer. Sean found out that Jesse had been using him to deliver drugs. He confronted Jesse in the house and said, "You don't care about nothin' do you, except your own greedy self. You don't care if they kill me, they kill mama. You don't care if school children use it. All you care about is yourself. As he pointed a finger at Sean, Jesse retorted, "You don't see me smokin' that stuff. You don't see me snorting it up my nose. Somebody has to sell it. If they don't buy it from me, they'll buy it from somebody else. So why not? And I don't see you leavin' this beautiful house that these drugs paid for. You know those clothes on your back, those are drug clothes. You know that fine car that I let you drive to drop off the drugs with, you fool, that's a drug car. And I'm not givin' it up."

———

Fourteen African American students at Howard University have been debating for the past three hours whether or not they should work for corporate America or work within the African American community. One of the students says, "You can't make no money workin' in the Black community. I got loans to pay, there's things that I want to buy, and I got to start with $30,000 a year just to break even." Numerous heads

5

nod in agreement. "Besides, I'm an engineering major. What kind of engineering work can I do within the African American community?"

Another brother says, "Man, you sound like Thomas Sowell and Clarence Thomas. Our communities are in trouble. You know every time we go back home it's like a ghost town. The same neighborhoods that produced us gave us teachers and a 'village' that cared about us. I've never been to Vietnam, but when I go into parts of my neighborhood it looks like what I saw on television; boarded up buildings, people hanging on corners. But you know what hurts man? What hurts is that some of those same brothers hanging on corners were my classmates. I don't know if I could just walk past them on my way to work downtown." Somebody else hollered out, "I ain't goin' past them. I'm not even gonna live with them. I'm gonna live somewhere else. I don't want them takin' my briefcase or my car on the way to work."

Part of the crowd makes a response acknowledging that they understand. Another sister says, "Don't get me wrong. See, I really care about my people. Maybe when I get myself together I'll contribute back to my neighborhood center, if things go right ten years after I got my house, my car, and a little money in the bank. I may even start a business in the community, but for right now it's all about money. I didn't want to major in accounting anyway. I simply looked at where I can make the most money. I mean I'd rather be a teacher or a social worker. I really like working with children or with older people, but I can't make no money teaching. For me, it simply came down to accounting, engineering or computers. Hey, I failed chemistry. I don't like computers, and I'm carrying a C+ average in accounting." She raises her hand and gets a "high five" from one of her friends.

Calvin Goldstein, a lawyer for one of the major Hollywood studios just walked in to the main New York City jail to post a $2,000,000 bond for 17-year-old Amy Fisher, who just weeks before had shot the wife of her 30-year-old lover. Goldstein knew this passionate love affair between Amy Fisher and the man of her dreams would make *Fatal Attraction* seem like a slow motion soap opera. It didn't matter to him nor his studio whether Amy Fisher was innocent or guilty and whether the wife would ever recover. Goldstein simply knew that Amy Fisher could not rot in jail for the rest of her life, even if she had to eventually return to jail, he knew that between him and his legal staff, they could buy Amy at least 12-18 months and that was all they really needed to replicate her story. This was a lover's triangle, where Amy said she was not going to give up her man, and no wife or any other woman was going to get in her way. Goldstein walked in and asked for the desk sergeant and while waiting for his arrival pulled out the checkbook and knew it was just a matter of time before the studio would be making a return on their investment.

Values/Materialism
Willie and the Folks were leaving the bowling alley about 9:15 p.m. Willie was a 17-year-old dropout and the Folks were one of the major gangs in the city. Their favorite colors were black and grey or black and silver. They always liked wearing the Raiders cap and jacket. As they headed up Martin Luther King Drive, about eight of them, this young chump, about 12 or 13 years old was walking out of the store wearing what looked like a Raiders jacket. They couldn't tell because there weren't any letters on the back. They increased the

7

speed of their walk. The young brother turned around, saw them coming and began to run. Willie and the Folks ran after him and caught him about a block and a half from the store. One of the Folks literally ripped the jacket off of the brother and began to run with it.

The Folks began to beat him. Willie stabbed him while he was laying on the ground. They caught up with G-Rock who had the jacket, but when they looked at it they realized it was not a Raiders jacket. The young man must have known that somebody may beat him up and take his jacket so he took the letters off. Willie, real frustrated, then cut the jacket up with a knife and commanded two of the Folks to take the shredded jacket and lay it over the dead brother. The rest of them ran off before the police arrived.

———

The Johnson family leaves their suburban home in their new Honda Accord. Mr. Johnson is going to drive and Mrs. Johnson gets in the car still powdering her face, putting on her lipstick, and touching up her hair. Kenny and Steve jump into the back seat. Kenny is eleven and Steve is nine. Before they even leave their neighborhood, they begin to play their favorite game "That's my car." Kenny points to a gold Acura. As soon as the Johnsons get on the expressway, while pointing at a royal green Bonneville, Steve counters Kenny's statement and says, "That's my car". Kenny says "That ain't nothin'" and points to a black Mercedes and they both say, "Woooooh, that's my car!" They argue for 3-5 minutes over it.

It becomes obvious that they no longer want the Acura and the Bonneville because they both want this black Mercedes. Rapidly appoaching the city, Steve notices a white stretch limo. He can't see inside because of the tinted glass, but he knows that the carpeting must be royal red and the seats must be as white as the outside of the car. Steve boasts, ''That is more than my car, that is my limo. You hear me? That is my limo.'' Mr. Johnson smiles as he begins to exit for the food pantry where they're going to drop off food for the needy and wonders, ''Where did they learn this game?''

———

Denise has not left her room for the past 24 hours. It's 8:00, Saturday night, and it was last night that she became angry with her mother. Her birthday was coming up next week and as usual she had given her mother a list of things that were acceptable for her to buy. Normally, Denise gives her mother three options, but on her seventeenth birthday, there was only one other thing that she needed, and that was a car. The past eleven years she had given her mother a birthday and Christmas list of things she wanted.

Denise began to look around the room and realized that she didn't have to leave because everything she needed was there in her room. She looked on her dresser and saw the telephone with her own private line. She then gazed at the TV set and VCR and thought about the video she needed to take back before she got charged for another night. She rolled over in the bed and saw her stereo. She was glad that her father, who no longer lived there, but felt guilty every now and then, had dropped presents off to ease his conscience. He recently bought her a stereo with a cassette player and cd combined. Denise got up from the bed and decided to put Queen Latifah's latest cassette on because she knew the ''Queen'' would understand.

Denise really wanted to go to a party, but didn't want to ask her mother. Selecting an outfit for the evening would not be a simple task. Her closet was much too small for all the clothes that it held. She thought about sneaking down the hall to get her Nintendo back from her little brother. She considered playing video games for the rest of the night. Denise hit the button on her telephone answering machine and played back the messages. She heard Karen talking nonsense and Omar practicing another one of his raps on her before he took it to the streets. She smiled and said, ''Thank God for my homeys.'' She grabbed a bag of potato chips and remembered that there were no more. She then laughed and thought to herself, ''Maybe what I need to do is ask for a microwave and a small refrigerator so I'll never have to come out of here again.'' She rolled over on her back and wondered why her mother couldn't understand that all she wanted was a car. She began to ponder why parents just didn't seem to understand young people and why her mother would deprive her of something this important to her.

———

I remember watching one of the Jesse Jackson talk shows and it discussed designer gym shoes, specifically Nike Air Jordan, Reebok and L.A. Gear. A gentleman stood up in the audience and said that he was a shoe manufacturer. He had made a gym shoe that was identical to ''the big three.'' A youth turned around and asked him how much it cost. He said, ''$39.95'' and they laughed at him. I decided that I was going to dedicate my next speech to this young entrepreneur. I was going to speak to a group of youth and have two pairs of Air Jordan gym shoes. On one pair I was going to take the labels off and remove the name on the shoe. I was going to tell the audience that the pair of gym shoes with the labels on it would cost $119.95, and that the other pair with no labels and no name would cost $39.95.

There were 150 youth in the audience and I had them all look at the shoes. Afterwards, they were to tell me which shoes they wanted. A hundred and forty-eight of them chose the Air Jordan gym shoes that retail for $119.95 while made overseas for $2.38.

———

It's 8:45 in the morning. They both had 15 minutes before they have to punch in to "the man's job." They both waited for the red light, but for some reason, it's taking much longer to turn green. Dominique is dressed in a wool suit, cotton shirt and silk tie made by Bill Robinson. He is driving a black Porsche. His belt and shoes are made by Jandieani. Natalie is in a red Jaguar that matches the color of her dress. Her dress was made by Dolce and Gabbana. Her leather boots were made by Code West and her earrings by James Arpad. They both look at each other and turn away. The light still has not turned green. They look back at each other. No, to be more exact, they look through each other and then they turn away. For some reason, the light has still not turned green. They then turn back and look at each other again, and this time with disdain, for they see each other. As they turn back away again waiting for the light to change, they wonder, "Am I Dominique? Am I Natalie? Am I Porsche, Jaguar, Bill Robinson, Jandieani, Dolce and Gabbana, Code West, and James Arpad?" The light turns green and they both speed off. Their questions went unanswered.

Herbert and Steel had a special kind of relationship. Their friendship started way back in kindergarten. They were both 21 years of age. They still played ball together, even though Herbert had played on the school team and Steel primarily played alley ball. They both had a lot of respect for each other. Herbert knew anytime he played ball in the "hood" that he would always want Steel to be on his team. The feeling was mutual. Herbert tried to play like "Magic" making assists and Steel liked to score.

Four or five years ago, Steel decided he was through with school and it was time to make some big money. He felt the only way to make the kind of money he was talking about was to sell crack cocaine. Herbert decided he was going to make big money, but he was going to do it through working with computers. Steel went his way and Herbert went his, but this afternoon they were back together in the neighborhood where they grew up. Herbert was home. He had just graduated from college and had begun to look for a job. For the first three or four weeks, it had not been easy. Everybody seemed to be impressed, but wanted to consider other candidates and "would get back to" him. It had reached the point where Herbert had begun to memorize their response. Undaunted, he remembered what he was taught in school, and sent a thank you letter to everybody that interviewed him.

Steel began to tease him and said, "Let me know if you're tight. I can loan you a few dollars". He pulled out a "wad." It was obvious that a few dollars did not mean what it used to mean when they were growing up. Now, a few dollars meant a few hundred. Herbert smiled and replied, "I still believe that my way is going to pay off," and Steel countered with, "My way is already paying off.'' Herbert teased him as he began to walk away and said, ''Let's meet back here every five years for the next twenty years and compare lives.''

In the movie *Trading Places,* when Eddie Murphy was poor, he was very destructive. When he traded places with a White stock broker, there was a party in his house and he became concerned about how his guests were destroying his property. This reminded me of the insurrection in South Central LA where there were families that felt they had no stake in America and joined their children in looting the stores. The insurrection in South Central LA reminds me of the night the Chicago Bulls won the NBA championship and people who didn't own anything felt that night was a perfect opportunity to loot the stores. Is there a relationship between ownership and values?

Values/Sexual Conquest

It was 4:00 in the afternoon--just one more hour and Raynard would be off work. He was already beginning to plan this big evening and anticipating how things were going to go between himself and Carolyn. He would start the evening off by picking her up and giving her a dozen roses. He was then going to take her to dinner. Raynard still couldn't determine whether the ambiance was better than the meal or vice-versa because they were both five star. This would precede a play. He was very confident that roses, dinner, a play, and good conversation would give him what he truly wanted and from his perspective rightfully deserved--her body.

In another downtown office Carolyn had her own plans for the evening. She had already decided to wear her "killer dress." The dress did one of two things. It either made men turn their heads when she walked by or it made their mouths come open because it was that kind of outfit. Carolyn also knew that she had the perfect figure to complement this dress. She knew the combination of this dress and her body would be too much for Raynard to handle. She had already decided that if Raynard acted right tonight that she would give him her "garden." Ohhhh, for sure, he was going to have to earn "it."

She had already decided that in order to get "this" there would have to be some flowers and dinner would have to be at a very exquisite restaurant. The play could be mediocre as long as there was good conversation dispersed throughout the evening. After the flowers, dinner, play, and conversation, Raynard took her home. They undressed and she looked into his eyes and said, "I give it all to you." He returned the look and said, "I love you." That was Friday night.

It's now Monday morning and Carolyn is in her office wondering why she has not heard from Raynard. Could it be that some men give love for sex while some women give sex for love?

Ice just took the final shot that won the game. As they were sitting on the side of the court, Ice, Skip and Keith began to talk about their sexual exploits. You wonder sometimes which one is more exaggerated, what brothers do on the court or what brothers do in the bedroom? They were all using the similar phrases to express what they felt about women. Skip said that he f_ _ _ _ _ the b_ _ _ _ for seven hours until she begged to go home. Keith, not to be outdone, said he has to wear earplugs because he f_ _ _ _ _ his women so hard that it makes them scream and it's beginning to affect his hearing.

Ice was listening to both of them and said they were talking s_ _ _ and said he met this new girl last night named Connie. He said he popped that coochy so good that he's gonna make it a record. Skip looked at Ice like he wanted to kill him. He said, "Man, that was my sister that just moved back here from New York."

Values/Principles/Ethics
It was the NBA Eastern Conference finals and Michael Jordan had a swollen wrist and tendinitis in his knees. He had not practiced the previous day and was not overly thrilled about warming up before the game. He even decided to reduce the number of interviews from approximately 100 down to 50. Of course, the major question that kept popping up was how was the knee and wrist, but more importantly, would he play? He decided that because he was tired and he wanted to give a very clear answer that would let everybody know how much he valued playing, the Eastern Conference finals, and his team, he looked the interviewers dead in the eye and said, "As long as I have a pulse, I'll play." He emphatically repeated his response, "There's no more need to discuss my wrist or my knees because as long as I have a pulse, I'll play."

It was Nelson Mandela's first visit to the United States after having been released from prison after 27 years. He was being interviewed by Ted Koppel who has a deep respect and high regard for Nelson Mandela. Mr. Mandela, the previous day had indicated that he

15

was very pleased to be in the United States, appreciative of the support and wanted the U.S. to maintain sanctions until all of the ANC demands had been met.

Earlier he had explained that while in prison and before he came to the United States that Omar Quadafi and Fidel Castro had been very supportive of the struggle for 27 million Black South Africans to be empowered with the right to vote. He stated unequivocally they were his friends. Ted Koppel expressed to Nelson Mandela that they are not friends of the United States and questioned Nelson Mandela on why he would support these two men. When Mandela did not denounce Quadafi and Castro, Ted Koppel literally pleaded with Mandela and said, ''But you don't understand, you're in America and it is not the most politically astute decision to make while here on your visit.'' Nelson Mandela looked him in his eyes and said, ''Mr. Koppel, you don't understand, I am an African. I am not a politician. Because I am an African I do not choose my friends based on my location or political expediency. Mr. Koppel, I'd like to believe that you are my friend, when I'm in jail, South Africa, London, and here in New York City. That's the way I feel about Quadafi and Castro.'' Ted Koppel looked puzzled as if he didn't understand and said, ''We'll be right back after this commercial break.''

––––––

David and Renee had been married for 11 years. They had four children and appeared very happy. David worked at the Ford Motor Company and Renee worked at an insurance company. They owned their home, went to church and attended PTA meetings together.

David would often tease Renee by asking her, ''Would

you stay with me if I ever got laid off?'' She would say ''yes'' and then he would ask,''Well, how long would you stay?'' Taking a quote from one of Dr. King's speeches, Renee replied, ''How long? Not long.'' Unfortunately, the inevitable happened and David was laid off. In the fourteenth month of the layoff, unemployment benefits had been exhausted and David has been looking for a job each week. He now has a much greater appreciation of what's required to run a household. He and Renee agreed that with his layoff there was no need to send the two youngest children to a babysitter. They could save that money because he would take care of the children and do more work around the house, including making dinner. The children could become closer to their father who when working was always away from the house for 10 to 12 hours each day.

David said it was becoming more and more awkward hanging out with the fellas. He was no longer a member of the bowling league, because it was somewhat expensive ($10.00 a week or $40.00 a month). He also admitted the difficulty of being a man without any money. David confessed to Renee, ''I knew when I first married you that you were a certain kind of woman. A lot of men believe that Black women are only interested in Black men's money, but I knew throughout our friendship that you were different. I think I teased you about leaving me if I ever got laid off because I knew that you wouldn't. I also knew that in this country at some point I could lose my job. I love you Renee.''

Renee caresses his cheek, reassuring him by saying, ''You'll always be my man. Ford didn't make you. Ford can't break you. Ford didn't make you a man. Ford didn't marry us. The Lord made you and ordained our marriage.''

One of the best interviews I've seen on 60 Minutes was with David Robinson, the center for the San Antonio Spurs. There were two major issues that I've never forgotten about that interview. Robinson was questioned about why he did not leave the Navy early and go straight to the NBA, or at least upon graduation, why he chose to fulfill his three year commitment versus starting his NBA career. He looked at the interviewer and explained, ''I gave my parents my word that I would graduate. It was the same understanding for elementary and high school. Secondly, I gave the Navy my word and they gave me a scholarship. I fulfilled my commitment to them. The 60 Minutes reporter shot back and said, ''But look at all the money you lost.'' David smiled and said, ''But look at how much money I'm making now.'' He then said, ''But it's really not about making money, It's about keeping your word.''

They went on to another issue concerning his Christian beliefs and how there are certain products that he does not endorse; and how that can be very costly in terms of additional endorsements. David responded, ''Well, that's true. My religious beliefs have reduced the number of companies that I will endorse, but it's not about money, it's about what you believe. I believe in Jesus Christ.''

_____

It had been a long political campaign. Jesse Jackson was in his hotel room. He had just laid down about an hour before there was a knock on the door. It was 2:00 a.m. He had strenuously campaigned in five states that day. Before the knock on the door, he knew they were coming for him. They had tried to get King and Malcolm

18

with the five White corruptibles: sex, money, White women, drugs and a position. As he walked to the door, he wondered who was knocking and thought about Senator Hart who had already dropped out of the race because of infidelity. He thought about J. Edgar Hoover and his attempted entrapment of Dr. King. He thought about Marion Berry and how law enforcement had used the combination of sex, women and drugs to trap him, and so when the knock came on the door at 2:00 in the morning at the Astoria hotel in New York City, he was not surprised when he opened it and saw this fine looking woman, with very little clothing, smiling, and asking him if was he lonely.

There were numerous options that Jesse could have chosen that night. He could have looked down both corridors to see if anybody was looking and invited her in because he was tired and it would have been nice to spend the night with someone. He thought about Jackie, his beautiful wife, and the fact that she's done a great job of rearing five children with his assistance. Jesse remembered their oath of marriage. He could have read some scriptures, had a moment of prayer and told the visitor that Jesus is real. Or he could have told her that they both know that this was a set-up and that as soon as he invites her in, the hidden cameras and microphones will become operable; and that five, ten, fifteen minutes later there would be another knock on the door and this time it would be law enforcement and the media. For all of these reasons, he decided to tell her to go home and keep hope alive.

Values/Trust/Honesty

It's a good feeling to be trusted. I drove to a gas station, I got out of the car and stood outside in the freezing weather to give my credit card to this indiffer-

19

ent cashier. I dreaded that she had to verify my credit status before I was allowed to pump gas. When I gave her the card she asked, ''How much did you pump?'' and I said, ''Nothing.'' She looked puzzled and explained, ''At this gas station, you pump first and then pay.'' I looked at her and thought I was on another planet.

I've begun to notice that pay first or pump first is based on the demographics of the neighborhood. I've observed variances based on how you're dressed and what time of day. I've even noticed that some of those trusting stations after 10:00 p.m. require that you pay first. I guess even in safer neighborhoods, management believes that there's a different clientele with different values between 10:00 p.m. and 5:00 a.m. It's nice being trusted, but it's an earned privilege that if abused can be removed.

I took my younger son to the bowling alley one day. We both had bowling balls. I had my own personal shoes, but we had to rent shoes for him. I was amazed that in this particular bowling alley renting the shoes was absolutely free and you did not have to provide your shoes for collateral. That is so different from some bowling alleys where you not only have to pay a dollar, which is almost the cost of the game, but they require at least one or both of your shoes to guarantee that upon completion you will return their bowling shoes.

An historical moment in African history was the negotiations between Toussaint L'Ouverture and Napoleon. Toussaint had successfully defended Haiti and had agreed to negotiate with Napoleon and the French Army. Unfortunately, Toussaint made the mistake of assuming that Napoleon shared his values and he was tragically surprised when Napoleon killed him at those negotiations. It reminded me of the African that took care of the injured snake. He kept him in his shirt to keep him warm and protected. When the snake recovered and was no longer in need of assistance, the snake bit him. It was a fatal blow. The African, like Toussaint, looked at the snake and asked, ''Why did you do it?''. The snake, like Napoleon looked back and replied, ''You fool, you knew I was a snake when you met me.''

———

Barbara proceeded to the cashier in the checkout line to pay for some groceries. She estimated $13.00 and gave the cashier a $20.00 bill. The cashier rang it up and Barbara was very close to being correct. The total came to $12.96. The cashier gave Barbara $37.04 as change. She hadn't realized that Barbara had given her a $20.00 bill rather than a $50.00 bill. Barbara is now aware of the mistake. Because her aunt works as a cashier, she also knows that if a cashier comes up short, he or she is responsible, either monetarily for the difference, or it's reflected in his/her evaluation. What would you do if you were Barbara and received 30 additional dollars?

———

I remember Jesse Jackson in one of his speeches at the Democratic National Convention describing how his stepfather and his brother would have to clean up offices. His stepfather used to show Jesse and his

21

brother how the owner would leave money laying around intentionally to test the family's honesty. If the Jacksons had taken the money, then of course not only would they have been charged with stealing, but they also would have lost the job of cleaning up the office.

Values/Identity and Self-Determination

I was beginning to feel a little ambivalent about going to my twenty year reunion. Of course, I was anxious to see all of my classmates. I had heard that several of our peers had died. I thought it was a really good idea for all of us to come together because none of us are promised tomorrow. I've heard so many people say "I know there's going to be a twenty-fifth year reunion and a thirty year reunion and I'll make those." My ambivalence was not so much about seeing my friends. I was ecstatic about that, but I wondered if my classmates had become Eurocentric and now measured success and identity not on who you are but what you own.

I really wasn't interested in going to a reunion if everyone was going to be interviewed with questions such as: Where do you work? What do you do? How much do you make? and What do you own?

As far as I was concerned, I'm the same "down" brother that I was 20 years ago, who now 20 years later I like to believe is a little wiser.

African Americans party differently than most European Americans. I don't know if we could call what they do partying or a networking session because when I'm in those settings, it's as if we're still working. I always feel that I'm being interviewed. When traveling, I've learned to turn the tables on those who ask the inevitable first question, "What is your occupation?" After I quickly respond, I ask the majority of questions because I don't want to be interviewed. If any information is going to be shared, the majority will come from them. I like the way African Americans, who are not class conscious, party. When we party, it doesn't matter whether you are a Ph.D. or on ADC. It's not about where you work, your degrees, or what you own. The bottom line is: "Do you want to dance?"

———

To me, one of the most significant episodes of the movie, *Roots,* by Alex Haley, was the dialogue between Kunta Kinte and Fiddler. Fiddler thought that he was free because he worked in the master's house and the master liked him. Fiddler really believed that he could be free regardless of the masses still enslaved. Kunta Kinte felt that freedom began with self-definition. He was brutally whipped because he did not respond to the name Toby. Emphatically, he kept telling his owner, "My name is not Toby, my name is Kunta Kinte. And you can beat me till I drop, but my name is Kunta Kinte." Kunta Kinte did not want to work in the house, he wanted to own the house. He felt that he could not be free until his brothers and sisters were free.

Values/Extended Family
Butch came running home from school during lunch and told his mother, Alberta, that Ms. Jones had pulled him by his arm and dragged him down the hallway, and pushed him in line. His arm was hurting. Alberta didn't like that. She didn't like anybody disciplining or chastising her children. She remembers all those days when she was growing up in her community and all the neighbors felt they were her surrogate parents. They not only would scold her, but they would also tell her mama how she had been acting. She promised herself

23

then that if she ever had any children, they would be her children not the "villages."

Alberta got dressed and went to school with Butch. Her sole objective was to curse Ms. Jones, and if the teacher didn't like it, maybe even whip her a_ _. Alberta arrived at school, didn't check in with the principal's office, and went straight to room 307 to confront Ms. Jones. Butch tagged along feeling real confident and cocky knowing his mother meant business and that justice would be served. Ms. Jones opened the classroom door and said, "Good afternoon, Ms. Williams." Alberta laid right into her and demanded, "The first thing you can do is keep your hands off my child. If you got a problem with my child, call me. You do not put a hand on my child. You don't pull my child down the hallway, and you better not push my child anymore in the line."

Ms. Jones responded, "Are you through, Ms. Williams?" Alberta sullenly replied, "Maybe." Ms. Jones continued, "It hurts me to see you act this way because I remember when I was your teacher. I'm the same way with your son as I was with you. First of all, Ms. Williams, you didn't ask to hear my side of the story. The unfortunate thing is I don't even know if you care to hear my side. Lastly, you've chosen to believe everything that Butch told you. Look at the way your son is smirking. Do you really believe I can teach him now that you've spoken to me this way in front of him?"

Values/Revenge

It had been a long night. The Cobras had one of its members killed just the night before by their arch-enemy, the Crips. An unspoken rule among the gangs was that "If you kill one of ours, we've got to kill one of yours". But now things were beginning to get

24

worse. The rule had begun to change and it was no longer an eye for an eye and a life for a life. Now, it was "revenge plus one." "If you kill one of ours, it now requires two of yours."

Flood, the Cobra who had been killed was simply at the wrong place at the wrong time. It was as if there was an all points bulletin throughout the entire neighborhood that a Cobra had invaded the the Crips turf. It was less than five minutes later that the Crips responded for that violation. The Crips knew that the Cobras would be looking for them. The Crips were laying low, but they were definitely ready and the Cobras knew it. The leader of the Cobras, Crazy Horse had already said, "We want more than one life, Flood requires two."

It was 10:45 p.m. and the police knew that within the next hour and fifteen minutes two Crips would be dead. They tried to round up as many Cobras as they could just to harass them and delay the inevitable. Crazy Horse had earned his name and it meant exactly that. He was half crazy and strong as a horse. At 11:41 p.m., it was announced that two Crips had been killed.

Values/Responsibility

My name Jawanza means "dependable". It was bestowed upon me by an organization that observed my characteristics. Those traits were developed by my father who, in my opinion, is the most dependable person I've ever met. He always told me that, "If you give your word and keep it you'll never be broke. You can take your word to the bank and borrow on it." That's why it's very hard for me to understand why people, specifically African American men, say they're going to do something or be somewhere at a certain time and default.

In our crime watch organization, Community of Men and in every other endeavor that I'm involved in, it is imperative that people keep their word. It is very difficult administering volunteers when people do not take organizations seriously and believe that "You should be thankful that I showed up at all." This type of behavior shows that they don't take the organization, its members nor themselves seriously.

Values/Maximum Profit vs. Life

An automobile company has just found out from its engineering department that there was a defect on one model of its cars. The engineering department sent a memo to the president that they needed to recall 175,000 cars that have this particular defect. The president reviewed the 119 page exhaustive report by the engineering department and their recommendation and sought a response from the accounting department. They explain that each recalled car will cost $300.00 or $50,000,000 in total.

In the engineering report, it indicated that the chances of a fatal accident were approximately 1 per 3000. A legal team is sought for counsel and they state each lawsuit will probably cost the corporation $200,000. The president has been taking careful notes on the implications from the engineering, accounting and legal departments. He knows that it will cost the company $50,000,000 to recall all the cars and 58 people are going to die if they don't. Those 58 families will receive an average lawsuit of $200,000 if they successfully litigate. That's a total cost of about $12,000,000. The president now has to make a decision on paying an additional $38,000,000 or accepting 58 deaths and negative PR. The corporation chose to let the 58 people die because it's more cost effective. Meeting adjourned.

There's going to be a very exciting summer rock concert. The promoters expect 50,000 people that will be seated. They also anticipate another eight to ten thousand that will be standing in front of the stage. This is called "festival seating." Some promoters nationwide have decided that they would no longer provide festival seating because of safety reasons. People have died like sardines, crushed by overzealous fans.

Many rock groups like festival seating because it "pumps up the crowd." Besides, who cares that an average of four people will be hurt one of which one may die-if 59,996 people had a good time? The 50,000 seats were sold at $30.00 per customer and the other eight to ten thousand festival seats were priced at $15.00. Everybody wins. The customer receives the tickets at half price and management makes an additional $150,000. Unfortunately, tonight it wasn't four people hurt and one death. Tonight all four people died and festival seating continues.

Clair Burton has been a secretary for a manufacturing firm for the past twenty-four years. She has had a monthly deduction for a medical insurance for all of those years and the company has matched the amount. Regretfully, Clair has just been informed by her doctor that she has cancer and that chemotherapy needs to begin immediately. Clair, overwhelmed by these recent events, wonders how she's going to take care of her two children. The doctors assure Clair that her insurance should be more than adequate. It's one of the top five nationwide in assets.

The following week, Clair receives the second piece

of devastating news. The insurance company has decided not to pay for the therapy. They have also decided that while this is the month of August, at year's end, they're going to terminate the policy. Clair is absolutely flabbergasted but enraged enough to take on the Dallas Cowboys, the Toronto Bluejays and the Chicago Bulls simultaneously, and still have energy to defeat this insurance company.

She wondered, "How can I give them my money for twenty-four years, for them to tell me that I'm now too expensive for them?" They really don't believe chemotherapy is going to be effective based upon their research showing a ten percent effectiveness rate. Clair continues analyzing her situation, "The only time I ever used the insurance was for medical check-ups for myself and the children and when my younger son had a fractured ankle."

To make matters worse, the company lawyer finds out that the most severe penalty that the insurance company could incur when taken to court, is reimbursement for the original cost of the chemotherapy. There will be no additional compensation. The lawyer also grudgingly informs Clair that it could take 12-18 months to reach a settlement. As tears began to fill her eyes, Clair looked down and responded, "I don't have that kind of time or money."

———

Mr. Wilson had begun complaining of chest pains and went to see his doctor about what could be done. The doctor gave Mr. Wilson an examination and an x-ray. Upon a return visit, he was also asked to review his diet. He asked him to try and reduce his red meat consumption. During a subsequent visit, a week later

28

after the x-rays, the doctor prescribed some medicine for Mr. Wilson. It was 30 tablets to be taken daily and each tablet was six dollars. Mr. Wilson had retired three or four years ago and did not have an adequate amount of medical insurance to pay for this prescription. He read about this medicine in a newspaper and saw on a television documentary where the pharmaceutical company sells almost the exact version of this pill to sheep for six cents each, yet charges humans six dollars a pill.

Mr. Wilson shook his head, but the pain increased. He looked at the wall and contemplated which pain is greater: the one in his chest or the one perpetuated by an American company.

———

Paul decided to take his VCR to a major retailer for repair. He was very much aware that this major vendor had been involved in a scandal with overestimating car repairs. He had also seen documentaries illustrating how companies would take TVs, VCRs, cars and other appliances, and escalate the cost of repairs beyond belief. Paul was confident that this major retailer had learned its lesson because this was their model, and because it's so difficult finding anybody to repair anything these days. So many companies want you to actually buy a new product. You almost get the impression that when they give you the quote for a repair that the sole objective is for you to simply buy the new item. They also want to keep the old item and use those parts to make another one.

Paul decided he could not afford a new VCR. The one he had cost $179.00 and he felt that it was something minor with the heads and that the repair bill should be somewhere between 25 and 30 dollars. Paul was correct. It does only need the heads to be cleaned. That's what the service man tells the manager who's working the front desk. Unfortunately, the service manager tells Paul that he needed a new circuit board. He also tells Paul that because he appreciated his loyalty to the company, while it normally costs $129.00, he will try his best to keep it under $100.00. He would basically charge him for the part. The labor would be free.

What the major retailer did not know was that Paul was part of a behind the scenes TV investigator team, and they had coded all the parts. When they took the VCR home, they were not surprised to find the same coded circuit board unreplaced.

———

Fred and Pam, who had been married for the past seven years, were on their way to the drugstore. They each had separate items to purchase. They noticed on the drugstore marquee that Jack Daniels whiskey was on sale and that no one offered lower prices for prescriptions and generic drugs. Pam went back to pickup her order from the pharmacy. She had been having a little stomach trouble and Fred entered the liquor department to pickup a fifth of Jack Daniels. They both appreciated that they were able to make one stop and achieve both objectives.

When are we going to understand that drug stores don't care what type of drugs they sell? If anything, one drug reinforces another. Purchase this drug when you want to feel good and purchase this drug when you're feeling sick. The bottom line is they will sell either drug you want.

Values/Ideology vs. People

It had been a long day. I had flown into Memphis early that morning from Chicago to speak for this school district from 9:00 a.m. until 3:00 p.m. on teacher/student expectations, curriculum, learning styles, and maximizing academic achievement of African American male students. During a break, two members of the audience came up and asked would I mind meeting with several people in the Africentric movement who were interested in exploring my ideas further. I told them it had been a long day, but I could meet with them for about an hour immediately after this six hour session.

They took me to this communal living environment where everyone was dressed in African attire. I had on a business suit and Kente cloth. I never will forget this experience because for the next three hours, they drilled me with question after question after question on how to improve the education of African American children. They also drilled me on the feasibility of educating African American children in America. I began to feel this was more than an informal session. This was almost an interrogation. While this experience occured almost ten years ago, I never will forget it because for three hours, this supposedly conscious community that said they understood the Nguzo Saba, never once asked did I want any water, juice, or anything to eat. More importantly, they never asked if I was tired and ready to leave.

I looked at these brothers and sisters who thought they knew the Nguzo Saba, and I remembered my grandmother, who did not know the Nguzo Saba, definitely couldn't spell it, but you could be certain that if you ever went by her house, even if it was an unexpected visit, not only would you be assured of something to drink, but there would be plenty of food for you to eat. If you had brought your family with you, they too would have been well fed. African and Southern hospitality can't be learned by memorizing principles from a book.

Values/Individualism

Today was the big day at Harlan High School - the academic assembly. Over 700 students had gathered in the auditorium to participate in a very special event. So many schools only acknowledge athletic achievement, and yet if a school's major mission is academics, then more glory and accolades need to be allocated for academic achievement.

It was disappointing that out of 700 students that attended the event only one student received an award. The program lasted 50 minutes. I began thinking the same scenario occurred with the Dallas Cowboys, Toronto Bluejays, and the Chicago Bulls. I was thankful that my bowling league acknowledges that if you bowled, you won. The trophy may not be as large as the first place team, but everybody played so everybody won. I recommend that the accent be on the collective versus the individual. Therefore, if a student advanced from one grade to another he receives an award. In this way, we increase the number of winners and encourage the peer group to buy into scholarship.

My name is Shik. It was a real nice dinner between the high school youth choir (Imani Ya Watume) and the elders from Trinity Acres (the senior citizen housing). There were about 40 of us and 40 of them. You know we wanted to talk to our homeys on the bus and in the

32

restaurant, but the ministers from Trinity United Church of Christ thought it was a good idea for the youth and the elders to get together monthly and talk to each other. I helped Mrs. Grandville with her plate and escorted her to her seat and then I went back for mine at this buffet restaurant. We were all supposed to pair off with three youth and three elders to a table. The objective was not only to have a nice conversation, but to interview them and find out what it was like during the era of the 1920's with Marcus Garvey, the 1930's and the Depression, and 1940's with World War II. At first, it was kind of boring, but I began to enjoy talking with old people. They say things that you don't hear from your friends. They like talking about their missing teeth, sore feet, and what aches and pains they have. I don't know if I could have endured some of their challenges, colored toilets and water fountains. They told me you had to wash your clothes on a scrub board. After listening to them, it makes me feel grateful.

Values/Violence

Ron was looking forward to leaving the big city and going to a Black college in the South. He was tired of the gang activity. He was with them sometimes, but tried his best to keep a distance by being out of town or across town. It was very clear that you're either in it or you're not. Whenever he was around the crib, he knew that he had to be in the gang. Ron said that he was tired of all the killing. He didn't mind ''whippin' butt'', but he wasn't down with the guns, shootings and the innocent drive-bys. As Ron made his way down South to enroll at an historically Black college, he was also looking forward to joining a fraternity. He said, ''Here we can still whip a lot of butt, but we don't use guns.'' Ron said, ''I know that when I pledge I'm going get my butt beat, but I'm looking forward to doing the same thing only more severe, after pledging my freshman year. I'm not worried about the national office and that nonsense about hazing. They need to come to the city. We'll show 'em about hazing. This is a piece of cake what we gonna send these frat brothers through. Yea, I didn't particularly like hearing about the brother that got tied to a railroad track at another school. They let him go at the last minute and he had a heart attack. You know when you stop and look at it, I mean in terms of gangs, they kill about 400 brothers per large city in a course of a year. I don't know why they're "doggin" the frat. You know, we may kill two or three. So this is goin' to be a piece of cake for me. Yea, I'm lookin' forward to going to college so I can kick a lot of butt."

Values/Sexism

The judge announced the decision "joint custody" for both Steve and Barbara McMillan. Barbara would have the two children Sunday through Wednesday and Steve would have the children Thursday through Saturday. Barbara was becoming more and more worried about this decision. She definitely wanted Steve to be involved in the rearing of their son and daughter. That's why she agreed to joint custody. Her anguish was in trying to figure out how she was going to raise her two children when she only made six dollars an hour as an office secretary. She knew it wouldn't be a problem for Steve because he was a truck driver and he averaged about eighteen dollars an hour. She thought that was unfair because she had two years of college and Steve was a high school graduate. She just couldn't understand why Steve made twelve dollars more.

It was fine when they were together because that really meant that they made twenty-four dollars an hour. She began to wonder whether she was going to be able to pay the mortgage now that they were divorced. The judge had made the decision for joint custody and therefore Steve would only be responsible only for paying his half of the expenses with the children. He would not have to pay for the half they were with her. She looked at the judge and began to wonder, "Why is it that men get paid more than women and why are my children going to be poor when they're with me and live very well when they're with Steve?" She walked out of the courtroom feeling dejected.

———

Sandra really liked Bill. They seemed to do everything together. What she liked most about the relationship is that they had a platonic relationship. Most people feel that men and women can not be friends, but Sandra and Bill had defied the odds. Not only were they the best of friends, they did several things together. They worked together for an insurance company. They worshipped together in the same church. They also were both involved in a civil rights organization in town.

This one particular day, Sandra looked at Bill a little differently. She began to notice that the insurance company was administered by White men. Bill seemed to take a very subservient posture in that environment. Saturday, when they worked in the community civil rights organization, Bill assumed a leadership position. The same thing occurred in church where he also was in a similar leadership position. While she was in the church kitchen cutting up chicken along with other women, she looked around and it began to bother her that these same Black men that can see White male

35

supremacy don't see Black male supremacy as it relates to Black women. She wondered what the reaction would be if she shared her observation with a girl-friend, who was working on the cole slaw next to her. Sandra took the plunge saying, ''Look at where we are in the church in contrast to the men.'' She had already been accused of being a feminist. She really didn't want to go through that hassle this afternoon. She loved her job, the civil rights organization, she loved the church, and she loved the Lord. It just seemed unfair that men were always in charge.

Values/Possessiveness/Ownership

The music was mellow and Luther was sounding better than ever. It had been a long day, Alicia was having a nice time at a very popular happy hour set. She liked this type of crowd because they were mature, you could easily assume all of them were working, and they all liked to party. Alicia enjoyed being at these gather-ings but she also was wondering how George would feel if he knew she was there without him. She was beginning to have second thoughts about George. She had always wanted a serious relationship but ultimately wanted marriage. She was concerned about whether she would have to give up spending time with her girlfriends, going to the health club, talking on the telephone, and every once in a while stopping here for happy hour sometimes without George.

As soon as that final thought settled in her mind, George walked in. He walked over to her and said, ''Why did I know you were gonna be here tonight?'' Alicia responds, ''I guess that's because you know me.'' George states, ''But why would you want to be here without me? Remember, I'm yo' man.'' Alicia says, ''Baby, I know you're my man, but I like being

36

around other people and you and I are together an awful lot.'' George replies, "But you don't understand, I'm yo' man. That ring on your finger, I bought it. That beautiful satin dress, that's my paycheck. You know that car that's parked out front, I pay over half the note for that. I may even have bought the bra that you're wearing right now. It looks to me like I might have bought the make-up and your panties. You belong to me.''

Alicia looks at George. Then she looks through George. Disgusted, she looks away and says, "Here's your ring and when I get home, I will take off your dress and your bra. I will also begin to pay my own car note. I will also give you your panties, but you can't buy me.''

Values/Racial and Cultural Pride

It was a beautiful summer afternoon in Monrovia, Liberia. The drummers had already begun to play and people in the village were eating millet and curry chicken. All the little girls had swarmed around Sister Mary, a White missionary that had been in Liberia for a couple weeks. They were all putting their fingers through Mary's hair. One of the little girls began attempting to braid Sister Mary's hair and every time she thought that she had achieved her objective, the braids would fall out. Right next to the little girl was an older woman and her teenage daughter. The elder women had no problem braiding Akua's hair and so the little girls asked the elder woman to come over and see if she could braid Mary's hair. The elder nodded. When she finished Akua's hair she went over and also attempted to braid Mary's hair. As she was sitting there braiding she began to explain to the girls that this is the "weak hair" and it's more difficult to braid. The little

37

girls began to giggle and say, ''That's the weak hair, that's the weak hair, that's the weak hair.'' Then they looked at sister Akua and said, ''That's the strong hair, that's the strong hair, that's the strong hair.''

Listed below are a list of values that were discussed in the vignettes.

Life	Work Ethic
Materialism	Money
Principles and Ethics	Violence
Commitment	Sexual Conquest
Family	Ownership
Identity And Self-Determination	Trust
	Revenge
Extended Family	Maximum Profit vs Life
Responsibility	Ideology vs People
Individualism	Seniority
Sexism	Racial and Cultural Pride

What I've attempted to achieve in Chapter One is to try to make the discussion of values more concrete. Oftentimes, we are not aware of how the decisions we make are based on our values system. Hopefully, we now have a better understanding of values and how they're expressed. We can now move into Chapter Two which is the most challenging chapter of the book. We will look at the external factors or Satan's agenda, where we are bombarded via the media to program our values and reinforce the value system of the oppressor.

For many of our youth, drinking and smoking have become part of their rites of passage.

CHAPTER TWO

Satan's Agenda

*"Money is not the answer to the problem
unless you have a value for spending it."*
-Maulana Karenga

The African American community and the Hispanic-American community are under siege by numerous forces. One in particular is the onslaught of alcohol and tobacco billboards in their communities. Unfortunately, many of the residents that reside in these neighborhoods are not aware of the disproportionate number of alcohol and tobacco billboards within their communities. Fortunately, there are ministers and community leaders that have begun to monitor this disproportionality. Some have gone so far as to mandate from these outdoor advertising companies that they either pull these ads down or they will be covered over with paint.

Under the leadership of Father Pfleger, Clements, Mandrake and others, a report was issued stating that just in the City of Chicago, in a 606 block radius of the Black community, the total number of liquor and tobacco billboards totaled 464. That is approximately one billboard per block and a half. The 464 billboards consisted of 339 liquor and 125 tobacco ads. In contrast, a survey of a 96 block area in the White community, the total number of alcohol and tobacco billboards totaled only 18; 11 liquor and 7 tobacco which was approximately 1 billboard per 5 blocks. In a more comprehensive report, looking at the entire city of Chicago which is divided into 50 wards, a similar comparison was made. The highest number of tobacco billboards in a particular ward was 25, with the mean of 13 throughout the wards. In African American wards, the maximum number of tobacco billboards was 117 with the mean of 36 throughout the wards. As it related to alcohol in the White wards, the maximum was 15 with the mean of seven, while in African American and Hispanic-American wards, the maximum was 111 with the mean being 38.[1]

It is naive for us to think that the onslaught of advertising in our community for alcohol and cigarettes has no affect on our consumer choices. African Americans are only 12 percent of the U.S. population. We only possess six percent of the income, but consume 38 percent of the cigarettes and 39 percent of the alcohol. Many of us may not be aware that while we are very concerned about the deleterious affect that hard drugs i.e., heroin and cocaine, have had in our community, last year 6,000 Americans died of hard drugs while 105,000 people died of alcohol and 434,000 Americans died from smoking-related diseases. Please note the following chart:[2]

Tobacco Kills More Americans Each Year Than Alcohol, Cocaine, Crack, Heroin, Homicide, Suicide, Car Accidents, Fires, and AIDS _combined._

Number of Deaths:

Tobacco	434,000[1]
Secondhand Smoke	53,000[2]
Alcohol (incl. drunk driving)	105,000[3]
Cocaine & Crack	3,300[4]
Heroin & Morphine	2,400[4]
Homicide	22,000[4]
Suicide	31,000[4]
Car Accidents	25,000[5]
Fires	4,000[5]
AIDS	31,000[6]

[1]U.S. Centers For Disease Control, 1988 data
[2]U.S. Environmental Protection Agency,
 ETS Compendium, 1986 data
[3]U.S. Centers For Disease Control, 1987 data
[4]U.S. Centers For Health Statistics, 1988 data
[5]National Safety Council, 1989 data
[6]U.S. Centers For Disease Control, 1990 data

Causes of Death
Tobacco vs. Other

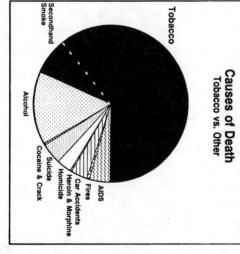

Outdoor billboard advertising is dominated by the tobacco and alcohol industries, with over 60 percent of all billboards concentrated in these two industries. In 1992, the tobacco industry spent approximately $500,000,000 and the alcohol industry spent approximately $150,000,000. Many of us do not know that the chance of African Americans-specifically African American males-dying from sclerosis of the liver is ten times greater than Whites. The National Cancer Institute also indicates that esophageal cancer for African American males was ten times that of White males; nor are we aware that 30 percent of all cancer deaths are directly caused by smoking. While the larger American population has declined in cigarette consumption, it is increasing among African American males.

We are naive to believe that we are unaffected by advertising. A recent study of U.S. high school students show that among high school students, who are regular smokers, there was a 61.6 percent recognition of cigarette advertising themes and 33.2 percent recognition among non-smokers. This high recognition is very important, especially when we begin to look very closely at children and teenagers, who like many adults are very impressionable. It has major implications when we are also aware that 90 percent of smokers begin in their teens and 60 percent start at the age of 14. For many of our youth drinking and smoking becomes part of rites-of-passage.[3]

In other books that I've written, along with other authors, we indicate how important it is that adults provide a positive and concrete rites-of-passage experience because gangs, media and peer pressure have devised their own formula. It often is not in the best interest of our youth.

In the cigarette industry, which kills more than

435,000 of its best customers every year, they must find new customers. They're very much aware of how impressionable young people are. One of their most popular ads has been Joe Camel, the cartoon camel from the land of Reynolds tobacco. The Joe Camel character plays the piano, races cars and wears dinner jackets and tuxedos, often catching the eye of a beautiful woman. During Joe's tenure in the pages of American magazines and newspapers, Camel has become the brand of choice for 32.8 percent of the smokers under 18.[4]

Values are by no means developed in a vacuum. Most people, especially youth, are not aware that the reason they do what they do, consume what they consume, and act the way they act is primarily a result of the onslaught of advertising that is placed upon them. Billboards are the tip of the iceberg. They along with print, electronic media i.e., radio and television, are extremely influential. Values promoted by these "drug" companies are not in our best interest. Their budgets exceed a billion dollars enticing young people at a very early age. It becomes a challenge that maybe difficult to reverse. Because I believe in the Lord, I know that we must do all that we possibly can to try to resist their influence. We need more ministers like Father Pfleger, Clements and Rev. Butts that have picketed these major companies and demanded they take these billboard down in our community. On several occasions, these ministers and others, when these companies did not rescind, painted over these billboards. In a recent court case, the judge upheld these ministers actions with the legal rationale being that it was simply an unfair practice for outdoor advertising agencies to literally saturate communities of color with cigarette and alcohol advertisements.

Ministers and community leaders cannot defend the African American community and this billion dollar outdoor advertising industry by themselves. Local governments need to do a better job of monitoring outdoor advertisements and at a minimum make sure they have permits. In an investigative report of how Chicago monitors its outdoor advertising, they noticed that 600 outdoor ads lacked permits required by the city building code. This was one-third of the advertisement in this particular community that was being monitored. Could the reason why this takes place be that in the city of Chicago, influential city politicians receive campaign contributions?[5]

We need progressive politicians to create legislation that will monitor advertisements in our community and see that it is enforced. It is economically and morally imperative that we understand that 3,000 young Americans each day embark on smoking of which one-third will eventually die.

Phillip Morris paid $350,000 for James Bond to smoke in the latest James Bond film. They also paid $50,000 to feature Marlboro ads in the Superman movies. They also have their Marlboro banners and billboards in children's video games. Phillip Morris lets candy manufacturers use its Marlboro trademark on candy cigarettes. Other countries are beginning to realize they need to protect their greatest asset, their human resources. Several Asian countries now restrict cigarette advertising. Singapore has had a ban on advertising since 1970. Malaysia does not allow television advertising. Hong Kong prohibits cigarette promotions on television and radio, and is now moving to enact similar restrictions in movie theatres. China implemented a stringent ban on cigarette ads that applies to television, radio, newspapers, and magazines. Pressure on cigarette advertising is also growing in Europe. Recently, the European parliament voted to support a ban on tobacco advertising in the European community.

Unfortunately, in America, this has not been effective because of the powerful cigarette and alcohol industry lobbies that contribute millions of dollars to buy politicians and influence policy decisions. This is another indication of values and the cliche that everyone has a price and that you can buy politicians very cheaply. This is a value decision that politicians have to make. It's between life and money and it's obvious where many have their values.

The alcohol industry, like the cigarette industry has had slumping sales. The cigarette industry created a new product, Uptown, that was geared exclusively toward African American males. Fortunately, ministers and community leaders were able to bring media attention to their neighborhoods and have this product removed. The alcohol industry has increased their ʾack on the African American communities. First ʾ was Cisco, a 40 proof dessert wine shoved next ʾcoolers in the inner cities. Now we have Power ʾmalt liquor that is 31 percent more potent ʾer malt liquor on the market and will be ʾe price as Heileman's Colt 45. An ʾsing campaign was directed at the ʾmmunity. Listed are the various ʾhol content.

ʾic Interest

46

MALT LIQUOR	ALCOHOL CONTENT
Colt 45 (Heileman)	5.6% (by volume)
Colt 45 Dry (Heileman)	5.9%
EKU 28	10.9%
Elephant (Carlsberg/Anheuser-Busch)	7.4%
Golden Hawk	6.5%
Haffenraffer Private Stock (Narragansett)	6.6%
King Cobra (Anheuser-Busch)	6%
Magnum (Miller)	6%
Mickey's Fine (Heileman)	5.7%
Midnight Dragon (United Beers)	6%
Old English 800 (Pabst)	6%
Schlitz Red Bull Malt Liquor (Stroh)	6.9%
Schlitz Malt Liquor (Stroh)	5.8%
St. Ides (McKenzie River Corp.)	8.0%
Turbo 1000 (Coors)	6.3%
Average Malt-liquor Alcohol Content	6.6%
Budweiser	4.7%
Coors	4.5%
Miller	4.6%
Regular Beer Average Alcohol Content	4.6%

Compiled by the Center for Science in the Pub

Malt liquor sales only constitute three percent of total beer sales making African American consumption levels of 30 percent of all malt liquor overall and an estimated 75 percent of one top selling brand even more significant. One marketing executive of G. Heileman Brewing Co. estimated that African Americans consume 75 percent of Heileman's leading malt liquor Colt 45.[7] Malt liquor companies target African American youth. A number of malt liquor companies have used rap music and other important cultural symbols to promote their product. Many purchase advertising on the nationally syndicated late night programs geared toward African American teens such as "Pump It Up." One commercial for St. Ives Malt Liquor uses rapper Ice Cube with rap lyrics that include, "get your girl in the mood quicker, get your jimmy thicker, drink St. Ives Malt Liquor."

With African American youth in many inner-city high schools involved in "40 Ounce Crews," youth, primarily males, get together and drink 40 ounces of malt liquor as fast as possible, listening to rappers glorifying Cisco, 45, and eight ball Old English 800. It is the latest attempt to exploit the alienation and powerlessness many African American youth feel in this economic and racial climate. A brochure for Old English 800 noted that the product is brewed for relatively high alcoholic content. Manhood is somehow equated with consumption of high alcohol content and wearing the popular 8 ball jacket.

Malt liquor companies have profited by targeting African Americans and Hispanics. While overall beer sales have dropped two percent, malt liquor profits have soared 11 percent over the past five years. These advertisements are not only geared toward our youth through the rappers, but they also attempt to secure the older market with Fred Williamson and Billy Dee Williams. One television ad for Anheuser-Busch liquor illustrates an appeal to Black consumers. Their ads star popular, macho Black actor Fred Williamson who asks, "When you pop the top, what's the clue?" A woman holding the tall glass of King Cobra answers, "Don't let the smooth taste fool you." Fred Williamson returns and adds "King Cobra gives malt liquor satisfaction. Don't let the smooth taste fool you." The message is that King Cobra packs power. The name and snake logo of the product reinforces strength. Five cans of King Cobra provide as much alcohol as six cans of Budweiser. Not to be outdone, Billy Dee Williams in much the same way in Colt 45, states "it works every time." In the ad, part one is the lady, part two is the Colt, now remember that the Colt is essential, and part three is a little luck. Well, I got the Colt and I've got my lady so wish me luck.

Because the alcohol industry believes they're an equal opportunity "oppressor," they do not want to ignore the Native American population. In their new product, "Crazy Horse", they've allocated two million dollars for product and marketing development targeted toward Native Americans. This 40 ounce bottle of malt liquor is named after one of their heroes, "Crazy Horse." G. Heileman Brewing Co. was so insensitive that when challenged on why they would name a malt liquor after one of the greatest warriors among the Native American population, they responded by saying, "We absolutely meant no harm by selecting the name. It is a tribute to a great Native American to name a beer after him." This again illustrates their values.

I've often felt that an excellent thesis would evaluate the impact that the ban of cigarettes and higher

Malt liquor companies often target Blacks-especially males-by advertising in popular Black magazines.

alcohol content products have had on the television and radio industry. For those unaware, tobacco companies and alcohol companies promoting higher alcohol content products are not allowed on television and radio. As a result, these two industries with sales approaching ten billion dollars have a very large advertising budget.

Consequently, they dominate billboard, print, special events and saturate television and radio with malt liquor advertisements. Just for a moment, I would like for you to look at any Black magazine you have in your home. I want you to count the number of ads and then count how many are for cigarettes and alcohol. You will be unfortunately amazed at the tremendous impact that these two industries have on Black magazines. These magazines literally would be bankrupt if these industries did not advertise in their publications. I also would like for you to review these magazines over the past five to ten years and see if you can find any article illuminating the tremendous health problems African Americans experience from alcohol and tobacco consumption. Isn't it ironic that the two major health problems in our community, lung cancer and liver sclerosis, are seldom analyzed in these major publications. Could it be that these industries control these publications?

In one of my earlier books titled, *Black Economics,* I illustrated that a full page color ad in *Ebony* costs approximately forty thousand dollars which most African American companies can't afford. These prices can be charged because there are industries that have large amounts of money that they can't spend in other advertising outlets and they simply outspend African Americans businesses. The inability of Black businesses to secure advertising in these publications is

51

secondary to the major issue that these two industries, tobacco and alcohol literally have the African American community hostage via its major publications. This form of slavery is not restricted just to magazines. They also control a large number of Black advertising agencies. These agencies also need to ask themselves where are their values and could they function without the alcohol and cigarette advertising budget?

While I am not going to list the names of these advertising agencies and their prostitution of the African American community, I do want to acknowledge that not all Black advertising agencies are without values, principles and morals. For example, one leading Black ad agency, Proctor and Gardner declines to handle alcohol accounts. Barbara Proctor, president says, ''I take advertising very seriously. A lot of people in this business say they only provide options for the public. I think that's burying your head in the sand. What we really do is generate need. The nature of advertising is to persuade - to create insecurities in the consumer, that only the advertised product can fulfill, therefore, I'm very careful how to use that power. I will not hype products that I believe are detrimental such as cigarettes or alcohol.''[8]

This is purely a value decision that Barbara Proctor has made. It has cost her large accounts, but it is something that she feels is imperative if you're going to live at a higher value standard where the health of your people means more than money. For many other advertising agencies, magazines, radio and television stations, her decision is simply out of the realm of possibility. Once individuals and companies believe the bottom line is profits, at any cost, then it becomes very difficult to change their decisions which are based on their values.

These companies have positioned themselves very

well within the African American community. Due to their inability to advertise on television and radio, and the disproportionate amount of money that African Americans spend on these products, and because they know many of us can be bought very cheaply, companies have positioned themselves to sponsor very important activities and organizations within the African American community. These programs include the United Negro College Fund, Black college football and basketball games, concert tours for entertainers, and jazz festivals nationwide. They also have award programs where they honor individuals within the community and give them contributions.

I was in a precarious situation, personally having been a Kool Achievers award recipient. What I did at the large reception where I had to give an acceptance speech was that I indicated the kind of destruction taking place in our community as a result of the consumption of the very owner's product. I got this idea from Mayor Washington, who in a Chicago election campaign found out that the establishment was giving out hams and other food products to African Americans hoping that they could buy their vote. Harold made a joke of them and told the African American community to "take the ham, the cheese, and whatever else they want to give you and vote for me on election day."

That's why it becomes very important that African Americans support those institutions that they feel are in their best interest. If we decide that the support of the 104 Black colleges is important, then we should not be dependent upon Anheuser-Busch to pay for the education of our children. If we value Black music, civil rights organizations and other important causes, then we have to support them. If not, then the alcohol

53

and cigarette industry will gladly do so. I thought it was kind of ironic that Carolyn Jones, executive vice-president and creative director of Mingo Jones Advertising, which is one of the advertising agencies that does represent some of these alcohol and cigarette companies was quoted as saying that Black groups are often so desperate for underwriting that they can't stand on principles. This is not only applicable for some Black colleges, civil rights organizations and institutions, but as was mentioned earlier, some Black advertising agencies and Black publications. In this chapter, as we continue to look at the external factors, the influence of mass media, and Satan's agenda on African American people, specifically African American youth, the next form of media that we need to look at is television. African Americans watch more television than any other racial or ethnic group in America. The Neilsen figures report that the average African American household watches 77.3 hours of television per week, in contrast to all other American households where they watch 50.1 hours per week. In spite of having a lower income than other racial and ethnic groups, 94 percent of African American households possess a vcr in comparison to the rest of the country where the national average is 70 percent. Eighty-one percent of African American households have cable television in comparison to 50 percent for the remainder of the country.

By the age of 16, the average American child has witnessed an estimated 200,000 acts of violence, including 33,000 murders and thousands of sexual encounters among people that were not married.[9] Please note that these figures were referring to the average American child. African Americans are not average viewers, because we're watching 50 percent more television which also encompasses more explicit shows on cable and video. We have to acknowledge this is shaping and developing values within our race that are not in our best interest. One study of a Canadian town that recently received TV reported that after two years of watching the new medium, aggressive behavior increased by 160 percent over pre-television levels.[10] A similar study in Belize, formerly British Honduras noted, ''We weren't ready for American television, and now we have things happening in Belize that we never imagined would occur. There are street gangs, guns, and shootings,'' commented the principal.[11]

The Institute For American Values reported that television content has changed dramatically since the golden age of the 1950s. Then networks were attempting to entertain the entire family. In 1951, there were 27 hours per week for children's programming; reaching a high point of 37 hours per week in 1956. Currently, there are no educational children's programs on network television during prime time, after more than 20 years of protests over ever-increasing sex and violence on television, and prolonged attempts to require quality children's programming. We can say with certainty that television content is worse than it has ever been. Many of the prime time movies shown on television today would not have passed network sensors even a few years ago.[12]

Neil Postman in his book titled, *The Disappearance Of Childhood*, indicates that the distinction between adulthood and childhood was based on acquired information. Adults had more information that historically was secured through print media. In today's generation, children and adults are acquiring information from television. Many children think they know the equivalent of their parents. Neil states there can be no childhood when there is no shame. Television is accelerating information being presented to children in a less qualitative manner. As a result, children are losing their childhood and shame.

The highly-respected host of the New York television show, "Like It Is," Gil Noble pointed out from his years of experience monitoring the news room that many producers have informed their staff that no news story should exceed two and one half minutes. The assumption is that an American's attention span would not allow information to exceed that length of time without wanting to change to another channel. I've noticed that in some homes there are four people in the house, each equipped with their personal television, all operating simultaneously. It becomes even more significant if the household has cable. In African American homes, as previously reported, 81 percent possess cable exacerbates the possibility of families watching one show together. While I appreciate the diversity cable provides, because it has almost no limitations, our children's values become further eroded and warped. Life was much simpler when you either bought a Ford or a Chevy and ice cream either came in vanilla, strawberry, or chocolate. Today, there are now 755 cars to choose from and ice cream now comes in 31 to 33 different flavors. Many households have 30 to 50 shows to choose from, and as a result, oftentimes, you will see dad watching ESPN, mom watching one of the movie channels, and the youth watching BET, MTV, or any other cable station playing rap videos. At some point we have to begin to raise the question, "Will 77 hours per week multiplied by 52 weeks, times 18 years for a total of 72,000 hours of television, 200,000 acts of violence, 33,000 murders, and 25,000 sexual encounters outside of marriage have any effect on the values of African American children and adults?''

What is amazing and bordering on being ludicrous is that the majority of Americans, specifically African Americans, sincerely believe they determined their values. They believe their values were developed internally and not from external factors such as media and billboards. People must believe this or they would be more selective on the external factors that are shaping their values. We need to admit that if we are concerned about developing a proper value system that is pro-life and pro-liberation, we then need to have external factors that reinforce that value system. It is naive to assume that we can possess a pro-life and pro-liberation value system and yet be bombarded with this kind of media blitz. For others unfortunately, they don't desire or are unaware of an Africentric MAAT, Nguzo Saba value system.

Many people think that network television is free. Many of us are not aware that commercials fuel television and that companies are very confident that in 30 seconds they can develop a commercial that will shape the buying patterns of the larger population. Listed below are the average costs of a commercial on some of the popular television shows.

NATIONAL FIGURES:

Arsenio Hall - $125,000

A Different World - $175,000

The Cosby Show - $250,000

The Olympics - $500,000

The NBA Finals - $700,000

The Super Bowl Game - $1,000,000

The networks are able to sell all of the time for these popular shows. There were companies that could not even secure the opportunity to spend one million dollars to convince you in seconds to buy their product. These companies would not allocate these monies if they were not confident that within 30 seconds they could shape your values.

Can you imagine what would happen if organizations that promoted MAAT and Nguzo Saba had the multi-billion dollar advertising budget that other corporations have that promote a value system that mandates materialism, individualism and competition? I've included three ads from the advertising council that may secure one page in some magazines promoting an African value system.

DON'T LET A HOT DATE TURN INTO A DUE DATE.

Just a reminder that one night with your girlfriend could last a lifetime.

THE CHILDREN'S DEFENSE FUND

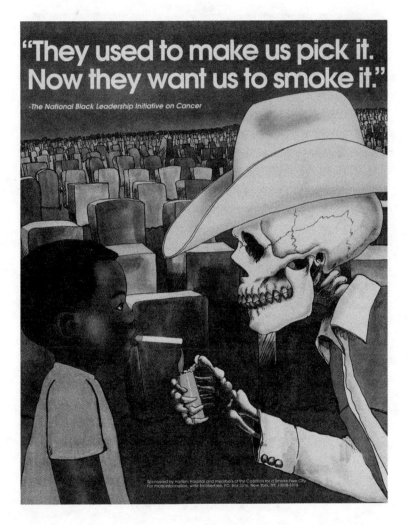

The white slavemaster.

When you use drugs, you're the slave
and the drug is your master.
So you're not as cool as you think...
...chump.

Addiction is slavery.

Unfortunately, the advertisement expenditure is far greater to consume drugs and to become sexually active than the response that we're allowed to provide. Please don't think that these decisions are only being made by European Americans on what African Americans will view. Black cable companies have the opportunity and potential to entertain and keep our community informed. The programming decisions are based on the values of profit and instead of empowering information.

If someone was visiting America and wanted to observe the interests of African Americans by reviewing the programs scheduled by Black cable companies, they would be very disappointed because the prime time line-up consists of rap, soul, and love videos, a Black soap opera, and a show reviewing movies and the lifestyles of the Black, Rich and Famous. A visitor would assume that African Americans like to sing, dance, laugh, curse, but are not very serious. If you want to find out about Black news, you could view that on Friday and Saturday. I guess the assumption is since nobody's going to be home anyway then that's when the news will be aired. Positive and informative talk shows that keep our community informed are moved out of prime time and placed early in the morning--the rationale being poor ratings. That's the same analysis and response that we get from larger White corporations that again point out that it has nothing to do with racism, it's simply good business principles, i.e., values. The value here is only about making money and it's not about trying to keep the community informed. There are African American presidents of large Black magazines and radio stations who make similar value-based decisions.

Many producers assume that the American population is only interested in negative news. Nightly news reports murder after murder after murder, and I just sincerely believe that if they provided a more positive slant on the news, and informed the community of some constructive activities that also take place, the ratings would not decrease.

This trial test would be inadequate if only executed for a short term period. It takes a producer and an owner who possess those values, but even after a year or two, if we still find that talk shows have lower ratings than rap videos, we should decide based on our values that the show is significant enough that we will absorb the cost of lower ratings. Please appreciate that this does not mean that we're operating at a loss. It simply means that an informative show may not be as profitable as another show, but because of our values we will keep the show preferably in prime time. How else can we change the values of our people? When I mentioned earlier that there is not one children's educational show on network television during prime time, it makes me wonder about the future of television, especially with the end of the "Cosby Show," and the death of Michael Landon who produced quality shows, like, "Little House on the Prairie" and "Highway to Heaven." These three shows in particular successfully attempted to instill values in children and adults that went against the grain of other shows by promoting family, communication, cooperation, respect, morals, excellence and commitment. These two men were able to influence television producers that there is a market for quality television that promotes family values. Unfortunately, Hollywood and New York are not convinced that the American viewer would watch these types of shows without a charismatic actor like the two cited above. We need to let the networks know via phone calls and preferably letters that we want more positive shows. Another major area of electronic media that we want to analyze and its effect on shaping values is the movie industry. African Americans, while only 12 percent of the population buy 40 percent of all movie tickets and yet only own one studio, Oprah Winfrey's television studio. We have no distributors and only one theater, the Baldwin theater in Los Angeles showing first run movies. When my company, African American Images, produced *Up Against the Wall* we showed it to Hollywood for distribution consideration. They said it was an excellent movie, but they said it was ''too soft.'' They went on to indicate that African Americans in particular respond better to R-Rated movies that are filled with sex, cursing, violence, and a generous usage of the ''MF'' word. They even showed me situations where the joke might not have been funny, but if the ''MF'' word was used at the end of the joke, people laughed.

I never will forget Bill Cosby challenging Eddie Murphy to tell a joke without cursing. Cosby took the position that Eddie was not funny if he did not curse. After a while, Eddie acknowledged that it is the usage of cursing that made him funny and he was not as confident telling a ''clean joke.'' In my audiences throughout the year I've been teasing them and asking if they could name one Black PG-13 movie made in all of 1991 by a major Hollywood studio that played in at least ten theatres and did not have Whoopi Goldberg, Danny Glover, or Tommy Davidson. I must speak in four different cities a week to a minimum of 2,000 people a week, and throughout that year, I only had one person to guess correctly. Hollywood is convinced that R-Rated movies are more successful and take the position that it is not racism, it is purely good business.

They showed me the financial records to prove that R-Rated movies like *New Jack City, Boyz in the Hood, Juice,* and *House Party* far exceeded the PG-13 movies which included, *To Sleep With Anger, Strictly Business, The Long Walk Home, Daughters of the Dust, Ghost Dad, Up Against the Wall, A Dry White Season,* and *Cry Freedom.* I remember when they were releasing *Living Large* and *The Five Heartbeats.* The commentary was they were worried that these pictures would not do as well as other R-Rated movies because they were not "R-Rated enough." Many of the producers said that the mistake with these movies, those two in particular, were they did not have enough sex, cursing and violence. Hollywood feels they have a formula that works with the African American audience.

Two movies in particular that really disturbed me and showed the kinds of values that are being given to our youth were *Juice* and *Talking Dirty After Dark.* In these two movies, *Juice* was simply about four Black males who literally killed each other and an unarmed, White store owner, and whoever was the final survivor had the "juice." *Talking Dirty After Dark* was a movie portraying a night club scene with the objective of who can outcurse the other. Hollywood spends five to seven million dollars to produce these movies and three to five million to advertise them. These are low budget films in comparison to their thirty to forty million dollar budget to produce and promote cleaner films for a larger White audience such as *Regarding Henry, Dad,* and *Dead Poets Society.*

They felt confident that they could spend ten million dollars on this low budget film and make twenty-five to thirty million dollars because African Americans are just interested in seeing themselves on screen. I agree with the individual artist whether it's John Singleton,

Ice T, Ice Cube, or any other artist feeling that it is not their fault if African Americans, within their audience, choose to act out what they see on the screen in real life. These artists feel that their movies should not be held accountable for this behavior. Numerous artists have pointed out that these people bring these values to the theater or the concert. While I concur with the analysis that some bring a decadent value system to the event, we need to raise the question, ''Were these people born with this value system?'' Since we know the answer is no, then we have to ask ourselves, ''Where did these people develop these values and do we want to provide entertainment that will reinforce this 'New Jack' value system?'' It is obvious that an audience who has members that will kill you because you look the other way, your cap is turned the wrong way or the wrong color, because you brushed up against someone, and on, and on, and on, should not be provided any media material that will even titillate these values. My wife often reminds me, while it is good for a producer or an artist to possess the ability to portray on the silver screen or in music exactly what we see on the streets, the question we need to ask ourselves is, ''why go to the theater when we could look right outside our window and watch the wild west?''

Then we raise the major question and that is, ''What is the ultimate virtue of art?'' Is it simply to illuminate what exists - a lack of respect for life, women, children, and elders? Or are we to take the audience from Hip-Hop to MAAT? Do African Americans that hate themselves need to watch movies like *Juice* where four Black males literally self-destruct on the screen? Hollywood says yes because their values are predicated on profit. While African Americans buy 40 percent of all the movie tickets within the African American community, greater than 75 percent of those tickets are bought by African American teenagers. These teenagers primarily reflect the Hip-Hop, New Jack generation. This group did not respond to *The Five Heartbeats* which was produced by Hollywood and had almost the same advertising budget as some of their other more successful films. *The Five Heartbeats* did not have a Hip-Hop, New Jack culture within it, while *Juice, Straight out of Brooklyn, New Jack City,* and *Boys in the Hood* did. I mentioned *The Five Heartbeats* as the acid test because so many of the other positive films like, *To Sleep with Anger, Daughters of the Dust, Up Against the Wall,* and *The Long Walk Home,* had a much smaller advertising budget. Many times the reason given for a mediocre response was the lack of advertising. *The Five Heartbeats* had close to a five million dollar advertising budget, but only generated seven million in sales in comparison to 60 million with *New Jack City.* Is Hollywood's formula correct?

The cleaner movies do much better when they become videos. The older audience within the African American community responds. If we're going to reach our youth, specifically our Hip-Hop, New Jack component of African American youth, we need to be more effective. I commend Spike Lee and John Singleton for providing a message within their movies. They realize that in order to reach the Hip-Hop, New Jack generation, in 120 minute movie, the message which may only entail 10 or 15 minutes must be buried in the movie. I frequently ask youth after watching *Boyz in the Hood* what were the three statements that the father told his son on what it means to be a man. Invariably, youth could not remember what those messages were. They could remember that Ice Cube always walked around with a large bottle of malt liquor, or how he responded to women at his barbecue party, or the fighting and cursing that took place during the movie. They remembered those things very well. Many of them even missed the most important message which was that the boy with the father was able to overcome the problems within the neighborhood that boys without a father were unable to achieve.

Ultimately we have to ask ourselves from a value perspective how do we want to be perceived on the silver screen? We have to also ask ourselves do we give the audience what it wants or needs? If the value is to make money then be assured that there will be *New Jack City* II, III and IV. If the objective is to inform and promote positive values among family members, such as portrayed in *Up Against the Wall* and *Daughters of the Dust* then we're going to have to begin to own studios, distributors, and theatres. We're going to have to demand more of our 40 percent market share.

The next area of the media we now need to investigate is rap. The research group out of Philadelphia Motivational Education Entertainment (MEE) has released an excellent report that describes the impact of some of the beliefs of this Hip-Hop, New Jack generation and what needs to be implemented if we're going to be successful in reshaping their values. The two major influences on this New Jack generation are "rappers" and the "peer group." The report indicates that 97 percent of all African American youth interviewed followed and appreciated rap music. Listed is a graph reflecting the kind of saturation that rap has in the African American community among African American teens.[13]

Black teens who like and listen to "Rap"
...between the ages of 12 and 20

Yes
97%

No
3%

Rap Music Preferences
MEE Report Statistics

1. Do you like Rap Music?
   97.7% Yes   2.3% No

2. How many Rap albums, cassettes, and/or
   CDs do you buy a month?
       12.7% 0   39.0% 1-2
       29.0% 3-4   19.3% 5 or more

The first thing that African American youth workers are going to have to do if they're going to reach African American youth and reshape their values is that they need to understand rap. Too many adults condemn all rap and when children observe this they notice the contradictions. The first one is that parents have never liked their children's music and that which they do not like is always too loud. Children notice that their parents play their music loud because they enjoy it. Secondly, when adults put all rap in the same category, it lets young people know parents are not listening to the words because not all rappers are negative. For example, list five positive rappers in one column and list five negative rappers in another column. Complete this exercise without referring to my list.

RAPPERS WHO USE POSITIVE LYRICS	RAPPERS WHO USE NEGATIVE LYRICS
MC Hammer	NWA - Niggas with an Attitude
Public Enemy	BWP - Bytches with Problems
Queen Latifah	HWA - Hoes Wit Attitudes
X-Clan	AMG - American Made Gangsters
KRS-One and Boogie Down Productions	Two Live Crew

When adults condemn all rap then they negate the fact that most of our youth are not wearing a Malcolm X cap and Africentric material because of schools or their homes, but because of Africentric rappers, especially the excellent work done by KRS-One, Public Enemy, and X-Clan. Heavy D And The Boyz have an excellent rap titled, "No Cursing." MC Hammer has a rap on BeBe and CeCe Winans' album called, "The Blood" (referring to the blood of Jesus Christ). KRS-One and Public Enemy literally teach an African American history course via their music. Conversely, parents are correct when they tell their youth they're listening to more than just beat, all the negative words have also been programmed in their computer brain.

Here are some examples of the kinds of lyrics that our youth are receiving from some of these rappers. On NWA's album when Ice Cube was still a member, there's a song called "Gangsta, Gangsta." Ice Cube says "Do I look like a m_ _ _ _ _ f_ _ _ _ _ _ role model? Life ain't nothin' but a b_ _ _ _ and money." On that same album, you hear the women in the background saying, "We wanna f_ _ _ _ you Eazy E." You can tell when a people are sick, when they can be disrespected and either are unaware, allow or enjoy it. On the soundtrack for *Juice* the major theme line goes, "What

70

could be better b_ _ _ _? What could be better b_ _ _ _?
What could be better b_ _ _ _? Not to be outdone, Two
Live Crew on the record that made them famous, used
their favorite line which was, ''Pop that coochie.''On
a song by the Ghetto Boys titled, ''Assassin,'' the
words are as follows: ''I sliced her up with a machete
until her guts were like spaghetti. Don't f_ _ _ with me.
I'm an assassin. Killed his teacher and his father. I
banged her and banged her until my thing got sore.
Don't f_ _ _ with me.''

The latest one that has received so much attention
is Ice T's ''Cop Killer.'' It goes as follows: ''I got my
twelve gauge sawed off. I got my headlights turned off.
I'm about to bust some shots off. I'm about to dust
some cops off. Cop Killer. But tonight we get even. I
got my brain on hype. Tonight a be your night. I got this
long eight knife and your neck looks just right. I'm
about to kill me something. A pig stopped me for
nothin'.'' This concern about cops is not new just to
Ice T. NWA had a previous song called ''F_ _ _ the
Police,'' LL Cool J - ''Illegal Search,'' Cypris Hill -
''Pigs,'' Boogie Down Productions - ''Who Protects
Us From You,'' and Public Enemy's - ''Anti-Nigga
Machine'' are to name just a few. It is unfortunate but
one of the things adults are going to have to learn about
the Hip-Hop, New Jack generation is that they resent
authority and it's based on an oppositional mentality.
So if the ''establishment'' has a problem with Two Live
Crew, NWA, and Ice T, sales are going to increase
while adults think they are developing a positive boycott for that particular song. For example, the sales for
Ice T's song ''Cop Killer'' were very marginal before
the boycott, but afterwards sales doubled. The same is
applicable to Two Live Crew. The Hip-Hop, New Jack
generation is not dependent upon the larger mass

media for promotion of rap. Within two weeks of NWA's album being released, 900,000 copies had already been sold with literally no radio airplay!

I am very concerned about the sexist, misogynistic attitude that many of these rappers possess. I'm not only concerned about the male value system but I'm equally concerned about women who don't seem to have any problem being called b_ _ _ _ _ _ and whores. I'm beginning to wonder if some negative rapper can talk about women without calling them b_ _ _ _ _ _. Many of us are unaware that MTV was founded as late as 1981 and has become a household word. They have added more rap video shows as they compete with BET for our youth. John Johnson also saw this demand and converted one of his radio stations into a 24 hour rap station because if 97 percent of African American youth like rap and buy 50 percent of all the music in America, it is a lucrative market.

Many of the videos that our youth watch in excess of 24 hours a week reflect not only a value system that is sexist and materialistic, but also portrays African American females primarily of a lighter hue. Numerous parents have written BET and MTV wondering if they knew that some African American females are darker than Vanessa Williams. Many positive African American parents have done an adequate job monitoring television, but are doing poorly with rap. Don't be surprised while driving your child to school and you're listening to the news, gospel, or rhythm and blues and you're child has their headphones on listening to either NWA or HWA. Every parent should monitor their children's music and begin to listen to their tapes together. I never will forget the day I came home and I began to play some of my son's music. I made it very clear rap played in my house needs to reinforce a positive value system. I also told them that any rap that contains cursing or disrespects women will be confiscated.

In this chapter, we have attempted to analyze the impact that billboards, television, movies, rap, videos, and radio have had on shaping the values of African Americans, specifically African American youth. At some point we're going to have to acknowledge that 72,000 hours of television, which shows 200,000 acts of violence, 25,000 sexual encounters outside of marriage, purchasing 40 percent of all movie tickets (among that group 72 percent of those purchases made by African American youth), watching an average of 10 hours of videos a week and listening to 20 hours of rap, the billions of dollars spent advertising liquor and cigarettes on billboards, and over 10 billion dollar spent on an ad budget between television, radio, and print has to have some effect on shaping our values.

Father Pfleger, Father Clements, Rev. Butts, Mandrake, and numerous others are making a difference. Our religious leaders are to be highly commended for their efforts namely, by reducing the quantity of negative media that is bombarding African Americans and at the same time, demanding positive advertising images, quality television programming and films. I have seen families write to the networks and have had shows changed or cancelled. I feel that Michael Landon did make a difference. Bill Cosby is still making a contribution. Behavior modification theorists teach we should give more attention to the positive rappers like MC Hammer, Queen Latifah, Public Enemy, Heavy D and the Boyz, X-Clan, and KRS-One. We will increase their sales and improve the probability that we will begin to shape the values of this current generation. In the next chapter we will begin to look at when and how the values of Hip-Hop and New Jack were developed. We will also look at how we can encourage youth to move from that point to MAAT and the Nguzo Saba.

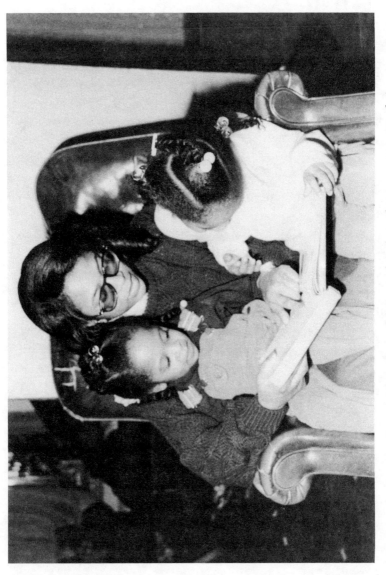

Young people are crying out for role models to explain how they can say no to their peer group.

CHAPTER THREE

When and How
Values Are Taught

"A people without values are dangerous."
--- Jawanza Kunjufu

My wife told me her Bible class instructor often says that if you are not saved there is nothing that you can do that would surprise him. He makes this comment frequently when students are reporting absurdities they saw on the news such as men stalking women, parents killing children or vice versa, multiple rapes and multiple murders. This is not to imply that those that confess God is real are sinless as evidenced by priests who sexually abused children.

We simply want to establish in this chapter that values require a foundation. Values have to be internalized and be a part of a larger ideology, a larger belief system higher than yourself. I believe the best place to anchor your values is in the Lord. The second highest source would be the liberation of your people.

An excellent article written by Johari Amini Hudson shows the direct relationship between behavior and values. [In the model listed] we can see "that there is no contradiction or inconsistency between ones true beliefs or values and what one actually does." There are no contradictions, or errors, or mistakes in behavior. *We act out what is in us. Nothing more, nothing less. What we say or rap may sometimes or perhaps often appear a contradiction or inconsistency to what we do. This is where the illusion lies. Illustration: If my rap is that I love my people and at the same time I am out in the street pimping some brother or sister, then my rap is a lie (as the old folks say, 'the truth ain't in it') not a contradiction, and my pimping is actually consistent with my values which are that my people should be exploited and hated rather than loved.*

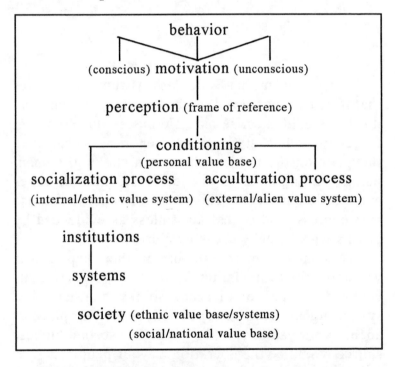

"Essentially a value base is the foundation of every society. As a consequence, changes in institutions or systems can take place only on a superficial level at best, unless changes have first occurred in the value base of the society. Therefore, changing an imperialist, exploitative economic system from capitalism to socialism would not retard or change their imperio-exploitative behavior; if the values of a society dictate that the people believe in competition, exploitation of others, and imperialism, those people will continue behaving in those ways regardless of their economic system, until their society's value base itself is changed."[1]

Julius Nyerere reinforces that values only require a circumstance to portray themselves. He states it has nothing to do with the possession or nonpossession of wealth. Destitute people can be potential capitalists - exploiters of their fellow human beings. A millionaire can equally well be a socialist; he may value his wealth only because it can be used in the service of his fellow men, but the man who uses wealth for the purpose of dominating any of his fellows is a capitalist. So is the man who would if he could. Two of the major economic factors that have shaped our value system have been how land is perceived and the usage of money. Julius Nyerere points out that land was not always owned by the individual and we did not always have an individualistic value system. The land used to belong to the community. Nyerere states that, "... in rejecting the capitalistic attitude of mind, which colonialism brought to Africa, we must reject also the capitalist methods which go with it. One of these is individual ownership of land. To us in Africa, land was always recognized as belonging to the community. Each individual within our society had a right to the use of land because otherwise, he could not earn his living, and one could not have the right to life without also having the right to some means of maintaining life. But the Africans right to land was simply the right to use it. He had no other right to it. Nor did it occur to him to try to claim it."[2]

In the acclaimed novel by William Griggs, *The Megalite Connection*, he describes how money was introduced to the society and it also has had a detrimental effect on our value system. ''These medallions are properly called coins.'' They are called money or currency. They are the means by which we all will be compensated for our labor from now on. This large yellow coin is a negapine. The second largest silver coin is a half negapine. The smallest orange coin is a quarter negapine. One negapine is the equal of two half negapine or four quarter negapine. From now on, whenever you do something for someone else, they will have to exchange one or several of these coins depending on the work that has been performed.

I have taken the liberty of drawing up compensation tables so we can see how much a given piece of work or item is worth in terms of these coins. Never again will you have to worry about your generosity being taken advantage of. No longer will your kindness be taken for weakness. Every individual and every family will be issued a specific amount of coins. Those of you who are shrewd (and who among you is not?) will be able to accumulate more and more of these coins. The coins will bring power and freedom. If you acquire enough of them you will not have to work anymore because you will be able to pay someone else to do your work.[3] As we begin to delve further into values, which requires a foundation, understand in the European value system, land and money are two of the major factors that promote individualism and materialism.

Throughout this book the attempt is to try to make values as concrete as possible. Gail Inlow, in a book titled *Values in Transition,* uses synonyms for the word value i.e., preferences, inner determinants, or criteria for decision. There is a relationship between behavior, values, foundation and ideology.

Therefore, in order to change the behavior you must

change the value system. It will be very difficult to change the value system at the gut base level if there has been no change in the foundation. Here in this chapter, I'm recommending that the foundation be based on a relationship with God and secondly a relationship to your race. Most of us are unable to articulate our values, their source of origin, and when they were developed.

This latter area we now want to explore.

Many psychologists and doctors agree that 70 to 80 percent of the brain is developed by the age of four. The brain cells of human beings are said to amount to 1.4 billion in number. Individual brain cells are separate at birth and they cannot function individually at all. At the approximate age of four the front part called the ''Frontal Lobes'' begins the ''wiring process'' where these brain cells are beginning to connect to each other. It is very significant to note that this period between infancy and four literally equals the development between the ages of four through seventeen.[4] It becomes imperative that parents not only provide a stimulating environment, but also breast feed, provide proper nurturance, and the proper value system that will enhance maximum development, especially between infancy and four years of age. This is extremely important because the first four is equivalent to the next thirteen.

The age of four is not only a significant period for the connection of brain cells, but at the age of four African American children have already been observed as being aware of the concept of race. Some are cognizant of the discrimination that exists within America. It is unfortunate that many parents and teachers do not teach African American children at an early age to have a positive appreciation of their race. This lack of direction in race awareness is also expressed in sex education where research indicates that a majority of youth are sexually involved at the ages of twelve through fourteen, while most classes and most adult practitioners don't disseminate information until fourteen to sixteen. Unfortunately, we are either late or non-existent on teaching cultural and sexual issues.

The next significant age that we want to look at is the age of seven. You've often heard the comment in the Catholic community that ''you give us a child for seven years and we'll give you a Catholic for the rest of your life.'' The number seven. The number of perfection. The number represents the cardinal virtues of MAAT, the seven principles of the Nguzo Saba, and the seven days of the week. The Catholic community is very confident of their capabilities with seven years. I wonder how confident African Americans are that if given seven years in an independent Africentric school, that they could confidently say that they would be able to give back to you an African American committed to the liberation struggle for life. I wonder how many African American churches are confident that you give us a child for seven years and we'll give back to you a youth who will acknowledge that he or she is a sinner, that Jesus Christ is real and they are saved by His blood.

The next significant age is nine. In *Countering the Conspiracy to Destroy Black Boys*, I looked at the fourth grade syndrome and the age of nine. This is a very significant period in child development. Children leave the nurturance of primary grades and enter into the detached task oriented intermediate grades. It is here in the intermediate division where there is less cooperative learning, more independent learning expected, content-oriented, less child interaction, and an increasing amount of peer influence, while a decline in parental involvement. All these factors obviously can and do affect the value systems of children. It behooves adults who are interested in trying to shape the values of their children to realize how significant the period between infancy and four and ages seven and nine.

The research group MEE states that studies on substance abuse indicate there is a window of vulnerability during the early teen years. The ages between 13-17 are when they are particularly vulnerable to outside influence and before their values and ideas have fully developed. Significantly, the onset of drugs and alcohol abuse is primarily limited to these years, peaking between fifteen and eighteen - while teens who abstained from dependency producing substances are practically immune to later addiction. Simply put, whoever influences youth at this juncture, will probably have them for life.[5]

Listed below is a chart on the major influences.

1950 UNIVERSITY OF MICHIGAN	1992 MEE
1) home	1) peers
2) school	2) rap
3) church	3) TV
4) peer	4) home
5) TV	5) school

The major implications from the above research is that youth are not listening in adequate numbers to parents, teachers, ministers and positive role models, but are listening to the peer group, rappers, and commercials. The impact of the peer group is so significant that appeals made to individuals to change their behav-

81

ior toward academics, promiscuity, or substance abuse are almost worthless. The most successful way to change individual behavior is to design the campaign to influence the peer group.

Young people are crying out for role models to explain to them how they can say no to their peer group. The current message simply says, "Just Say No!" but seldom is there a program that explains how to do it within the context of a very influential peer group. If you're speaking to a group of youth about substance abuse or sexuality, simply sharing with the group the importance of abstaining is not enough because the individual has to explain his or her behavior to their peer group. Consequently, an effective role model has got to find influential ways to impact the peer group.

An example of how this has been done in other parts of the world is an Australian campaign ad where a bunch of girls are talking together about boys who drink. A member of the group says, "I think guys who drink are Johnny's. They're barffed. I think he's real stupid. It's just really disgusting. I don't think he's attractive at all." Then you sit back and listen to this and say" Well G, maybe girls don't think this is cool."

At the age of 18, if we have successfully done our job between infancy and four years of age, the ages 7, 9, and 13-18, then the onslaught of peer pressure and media won't be as disturbing. We should have young people with virtues that include what Val Jordan has developed in the Black value system. They include:

1) A Commitment to God
2) A Commitment to the Black Community
3) A Commitment to the Black Family
4) Dedication to the Pursuit of Education

5) Dedication to the Pursuit of Excellence
6) An Adherence to the Black Work Ethic
7) A Commitment to Self-Discipline and Self-Respect
8) A Disavowal of the Pursuit of Middle Classness
9) Pledge to Make the Fruits of All Developing Acquired Skills Available to the Black Community
10) Pledge to Allocate Regularly a Portion of Personal Resources for Strengthening and Supporting Black Institutions
11) Pledge Allegiance to all Black Leadership who Espouse and Embrace the Black Value System
12) A Personal Commitment to Embracement of the Black Value System to Measure the Worth and Validity of all Activity in Terms of Positive Contributions to the General Welfare of the Black Community and the Advancement of Black People Towards Freedom

The question we need to ask ourselves is how effective have we been between infancy and 18 at instilling these values in our youth. If we have been unsuccessful, what can we do with a person whose value system is 80 to 90 percent developed by the age of 18? What can we do to convert a value system where "I" is more important than "we", competition is better than cooperation, and materialism is better than MAAT and the Nguzo Saba?

There are several theories that I want to share and the first one is from Robert Merton on anomie (the theory to explain the adaptation of individuals who may not be able to meet the acceptable goals of the society). Merton's theory of social adjustment includes conformity, innovation, retreatism, ritualism, and rebellion. Listed below is a model.[6]

	CULTURE GOALS	INSTITUTIONALIZED MEANS
Conformity	+	+
Innovation	+	-
Retreatism	-	-
Ritualism	-	+
Rebellion	+ -	+ -
+ = Acceptance		
- = Rejection		
+ - = Rejection of prevailing values and the substitute of new values		

In the area of conformity, the person accepts the values of the society and has the legal means to be successful. A White boy with a high school diploma that makes more than anyone else in America with a college degree, won't have difficulty conforming to those values. An African American who has been given high expectations by teachers and parents and has access to funding for college and employment will also in all probability conform. The second component is innovation where the person has accepted the goals and values of the society, but has not been given the legal means to secure those goals. Therefore, a person who values owning a Mercedes or BMW, but reads below the sixth grade level may resort to other ways to secure that level of income: i.e. drugs, crime, sports, music, or the lottery. Retreatism is the expression of the individual to simply drop out of society all together. They don't buy into the goals of the society, nor do they buy into the means to pay for it. This can best be expressed by people that voluntarily choose to be homeless and unemployed. Ritualism can best be expressed by people who have been beaten by the system,

84

and now have decided that in order to function adequately, they have lowered their expectations and have less desire to accumulate what society feels is success i.e., cars, clothes, and houses and have found a legal way to finance their lifestyles. Some people are content with making minimum wage and have lowered their desired standard of living.

The last component of Merton's theory is rebellion. This is where the individual not only does not accept the values of society, they also do not believe they have to accept 12 to 16 years of miseducation and work 40 hours a week to maintain someone else's desire for success.

There are many African American youth operating either in the mode of innovation or rebellion. In order for them to make this transition successfully, they need adults who will explain to them that you do not have to accept this present value system, but you do need to replace it with something that is God-centered and Africentric. I'd like for the reader to ask themselves where they are and their youth in Merton's theory. In South Central LA, those people that were looking for any reason to loot a store and were involved in the riot, in Merton's theory that would be the innovation stage. Those people that burned Korean liquor stores and/or facilitated a truce with the gangs were involved in an insurrection and in Merton's theory would be called a rebellion. They did not accept America's value system, nor did they accept America's way of achieving it. This is very important, especially for the public and private officials people who think that the way to solve the problems of South Central LA and any other area is to simply drop money into the city. That reinforces the value of conformity. People that believe that don't understand the value system of rebellion.

In talking with many of the gang members in South Central LA and reading as much literature as I could about that situation, one gang member was quoted as saying "The churches could do more. I'll be in a mall with a couple of my homeys and we'll see some church people there. They'll say, 'Excuse me brother. Can I talk to you for a minute about Jesus?' And they always grab on to someone who's real clean cut to witness Jesus about. You know what I'm sayin'? And then here we come. But they won't say nothin' to us. Won't even get caught lookin' at us. So I walk up on em and I say, 'How bout me. I'm not worthy of God? How come y'all don't witness to me?'"[7]

That's why I really appreciate the words of Sam Procter when he expressed, "Not long ago, I visited a New Jersey prison to speak at their program. In my conversations with the inmates, it was clear that it was about the age of 16 that they found their awareness of their freedom was unmatched by sufficient moral grooming and education, and that the unstructured adult world was mined with more challenges that they failed to handle successfully." One said to me 'Man, if I had met anybody to talk to me when I was 16, like you did today, I wouldn't be here in this place for the rest of my life.'[8]

If we're going to be successful in trying to change the value system of young people who are now 18 and older, and move them to the value system of MAAT and the Nguzo Saba, we can't ignore them.

Ideally speaking, we have an 80 percent chance for success rate if we can reach young people between infancy and 18. There is still a 20 percent possibility that we can convert people from New Jack and Hip-Hop to the Nguzo Saba and MAAT in the latter years. I not only have my faith to rely on but I also have the example of the conversion process that took place within the life of Malcolm Little to Detroit Red to Malcolm X to El Hajj Malik El-Shabazz.

There are so many dimensions to Malcolm. I think Ozzie Davis said it so elegantly, "He brought out the best in all of us and especially in Black men, because he represented so many of us in different stages of our lives." Malcolm was always growing and developing. Unlike so many of the 609,000 African American males that are "doing time" in prison, Malcolm "used time" and read the dictionary cover to cover along with numerous other books and developed himself.

The Malcolm model is very important for youth and social workers, and other professionals that are burning out and becoming frustrated on whether it's even possible to change an adolescent's value system. For that reason my company, African American Images and our curriculum SETCLAE have designed the Malcolm X classroom that will replace out of school suspension with in-house suspension. We feel that there is very little development that takes place in a three to five day out of school suspension. Just as with the Merton model, I'd like for the reader to ask him or herself which stage on Cross's model listed below is he or she presently. I also want you to think about the youth that you're working with and where they are within this model as well.

Malcolm

This Malcolm X classroom experience is similar to the program Scared Straight. It encompasses field trips to prisons, the morgue, public hospitals (midnight on Saturday), and drug abuse programs. It also includes cultural books and videos and provides role playing from a street perspective along with curriculum mate-

rials that are developed through SETCLAE. The life of
Malcolm X can easily fall into the Cross model of
Nigrescense or the Negro to Black conversion model
or what presently is called the search for Africentricity
(the five stages of Black identity development). These
stages include the pre-encounter (depicts the identity
to be changed), encounter (isolates the point in which
the person feels compelled to change), immersion (describes the vortex of identity change), internalization
(expresses the usage of information acquired), and
commitment (a long term expression of internalization
and a commitment to the entire human race).[9]

Pre-encounter --- Malcolm Little / Detroit Red

Encounter -------- Prison

Immersion -------- The Interaction with Elijah
                          Muhammad and Reading

Internalization -- Minister

Commitment ----- Mecca

One of the best conversion models that I've seen
comes out of South Central LA titled, The Gang
Classes. It is a ten week course for gang members that
are in juvenile detention. The first thing that the students are asked to do is to write their own obituary
along with a letter to their mothers explaining why it
was necessary for them to die for the gangs.

For many of our youth they simply are not given an
opportunity to see the relationship between their behavior and values and the implications that it has for
their families and the victim's family. Many youth have
changed their values after the above experiences. For
the hard core, this may not be enough.

The most significant part of the class is the exercise
called, The Kill. The adult coordinator Mr. Jones
writes on the chalkboard the word "kill" and then he

says, "Now, I want each of you to give me a real good reason to kill somebody." The words are barely out of his mouth when hands begin to jab the air. Jones nods at one of the kids who replies, "For the f _ _ _ of it." Jones turns back to the blackboard, writes the words and says "Ok, for the f _ _ _ of it. Let's have another reason." Another student suggests, "Put in work for the hood." Jones writes again and says, "Ok, that's a good reason." Next student says, "Cause he's my enemy." "Yea, that's righteous," Jones prints quickly 'an enemy.' Another student calls out, "For revenge." "Yea, let's get that one down. That's a good one - revenge." "Cause he said somethin' wrong." Jones needing clarity asked, "You mean like 'dissed you?" "Naw, just wrong. Like you know, wrong." Jones pursued a definitive answer, "Because he said something wrong and now you got to smoke 'em for it right." "Yea." The kid slouches back in his chair grinning. He is clearly well pleased with himself for having made his thoughts so perfectly understood.

Jones writes the words on the board then turns back to face the kids and says, "Come on, let's get some reasons up here. Y'all supposed to be such tough dudes. Let's go." Now the answers begin to come quickly: "Cause he looked at me funny," "Gimme that mad dog look," "Cause I don't like him," "Cause he wearing the wrong color," "Cause he gonna hurt a member of my family for money," Jones just nods his head, scribbling furiously on the blackboard. "So I can jack somebody for dope," "Cause he give me no respect," "Cause he a disgrace," "He a buster," "For his car," "Cause he try to get with my lady," "Cause he a spy in my hood," "In self-defense," "Cause he try to jack you and take yo' sh _ _ for a nickel," "For the way he walk," "If he got somethin' I want and he don't wanna give it to me," "Cause I'm a lock," "For his association," "Cause he call me a baboon - dissed me," "Cause he f_ _ _ _ with my food - you know like took one of my french fries," "Cause I don't like his attitude," "Cause he say the wrong things - he woofed me," "Cause I'm buzzed - you know like high and bent," "Just playin' around," "Cause he f_ _ _ _ _ up my hair in the barber shop."

Jones chuckles as he writes down, "F_ _ _ _ _ up your hair, huh? Well I can understand that." The reasons keep coming. "Cause he a snitch," "Cause he hit up my wall - crossing out names and sh_ _ writing RIP," "If a lady don't give me what I want - you know the wild thing," "Cause they ugly," "Cause he try to run a con on me." All of the reasons are on the board in three neatly lettered rows. Mr. Jones steps back surveying the list for a moment, nodding his head. Then he turns to look at the kids again and says "Ok, now which of this sh_ _ would you die for?" There is a moment of utter silence. The air seems to freeze with the combined stares of shocked students. Jones stands quietly staring back at them, then challenges them, "Aw, come on now. If all y'all can kill for somethin,' y'all better be ready to die for it. So let's hear it. Which of these reasons you gon' die for? One of the kids pipes up and say "Hell, you can erase all that sh_ _" "No, let's go point by point," Jones responds. He continues the challenge. Back at the blackboard, Jones examines the list, "See what we got here. Ok. Who's gonna die for the f_ _ _ of it?"

As Jones goes over each item that they would be willing to die for, they erase all but three that they would kill for. They agreed they would die for their family, for self-defense, and for the gang. Jones then says, "Let me tell you somethin, you can be down for your hood. You can go to jail for your hood. You can die for your hood. If you do, if you die, you know what happens, nothin'. Nothin' changes. The beat goes on. All your dead homeboys, even they don't mean diddly because nothin' changes.'' Then Mr. Jones puts on the board the words ''irrational'' and ''normal.'' He says most normal people have a kill - die equation. What they would kill for is what they would die for. For an irrational person there's no relationship in the kill - die equation. One of the younger kids, the one who was ready to kill the barber for a less than satisfactory hair cut pipes up, ''How many numbers was on that black board?'' Jones informed him and the class, ''Y'all gave thirty-seven reasons to kill.'' The kid shakes his head and says ''Thirty-seven is a big a_ _ number.'' He agrees with the student, ''Yea it is and if you got more than two reasons then you're more than irrational.'' ''You're crazy.''[10]

The last conversion model I want to look at is where you list the ten sources that you value. List them first and then review the list from number ten through number one so that you can see what is it that you value more than anything else.

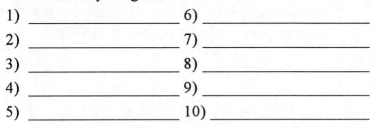

1) _____   6) _____

2) _____   7) _____

3) _____   8) _____

4) _____   9) _____

5) _____   10) _____

Many of the sources that people use for their top ten to fifteen are friends, sex, life, car, clothes, money, God, education, house, business, health, and family. Oftentimes we really don't know what it is that we value and only when we are forced to make choices do we find out where our values lie. There is a direct relationship between values and behavior. It behooves all of us to have a better understanding of where our values are and also to try to improve the value system of the young people and adults we interact with on a daily basis. The criteria of what it is that we value, as mentioned earlier, is tied to a foundation.

Values have to be rooted in a foundation and behavior is an expression of that value system. The criteria that was probably used to make the decision on ranking what it was that we value not only comes out of foundation, it also comes out of a psychological framework.

Wade Nobles points out that the distinction between African psychology and European psychology is very clear. African psychology relates to the concept of being and becoming. The African idea is relevant to these two concerns that are found in the beliefs that 1. human beings in society are governed by divine inspiration and 2. the process of becoming is governed by the notion of the compliment of difference.[11] Linda Meyers substantiates this concept of an ancient Africentric psychology by classifying African psychology as being ''optimal'' and European psychology as being ''suboptimal.'' Listed are her classifications.

Conceptual Systems

Assumptions	Optimal	Sub-optimal
Ontology (nature of reality)	Spiritual (known in an extrasensory fashion) and material (known through the five senses) as one	Material with possible spiritual aspect that is separate and secondary
Epistemology (nature of knowledge)	Self-knowledge known through symbolic imagery and rhythm	External knowledge known through counting and measuring
Axiology (nature of value)	Highest value in positive interpersonal relationships among people	Highest value in objects or acquisition of objects
Logic (reason)	Diunital-emphasize union of opposites (both/and conclusions)	Dichotomous-emphasize duality (either/or conclusions)
Process	Ntuology-all sets are interrelated through human and spiritual networks	Technology-all sets are repeatable and reproducible
Identity	Extended self, multi-dimensional	Individual form
Self-worth	Intrinsic in being criteria or materialism	Based on external
Values guiding behavior	Spiritualism, oneness with nature, communalism	Materialism, competition, individualism
Sense of well-being	Positively consistent despite appearance due to relationship with source	In constant flux and struggle
Life-space	Infinite and unlimited (spirit manifesting)	Finite and limited (beginning with birth and ending with death)

The exemplary work of Wade Nobles, Linda Meyers, Na'im Akbar, Daudi Azibo, Joseph Baldwin, Robert Williams, and numerous other Black psychologists give us a firm grounding on the understanding of African psychology. This is a psychology where spirituality is primary and then materialism is of less significance. African psychology produces people that are secure, who are in harmony with people and with nature, and look for similarities and are comfortable with differences. John Mbiti reinforces this African psychology with the relationship with God. The extended family is paramount to the extent that identity is not predicated on what you own, but your relationship with God and Mbiti is often quoted, "I am because we are" which is succinctly African.

People with a European value system that is grounded and rooted in European psychology have a value system that expresses, "I am because of what I own." This is best expressed when you go to parties and happy hours and in a casual conversation people will ask where do you work, what do you do, how much do you own, where do you live, and what do you drive all while they're observing your attire. This information will let them know whether it is worth pursuing a conversation with you. Can you imagine being in that kind of setting possessing an Africentric world view and an Africentric value based on the Nguzo Saba and MAAT? When being queried, I simply respond with "I am because we are and I am God's child. It has nothing to do with my Ph.D., I'm a sinner saved by His blood. I am because we are. I am Eddie and Mary's child. My wife's name is Rita. My sister's name is Cynthia. My pastor's name is Jeremiah." I am because we are and because we are an extended family (in fictive kinship) then you are my brother or my sister. Your problems are my problems and my problems are your problems.

I marvel when I'm with someone White and I'll ask, "How are you doing, brother?" or "How are you doing, sister?" and Whites that don't understand the culture are really blown away because they don't understand how we're using that term. An Africentric value system implores that type of relationship. Unfortunately, many of us are beginning to lose that value system and when we find out that someone in our fictive kinship is getting a divorce, lost his job, on drugs, or having some problems, we begin to take a standoffish attitude. We say that it's, "really none of my business." Unfortunately, often the victims also believe that it's none of your business.

I've always been concerned about 200 people attending a wedding and the couple can't find two people to be involved in a reconciliation. That's not African. This African psychology has its roots, foundation, and origin in what the Greeks call the "Egyptian Mystery System." What was a mystery to them was to the Egyptians the Grand Lodge of Wa'at. It was at this first university that the major virtues of Africentricity were taught.

They included 1. control of thought, 2. control of action, 3. devotion of purpose, 4. faith in the master's ability to teach the truth, 5. faith in ones ability to assimilate the truth, 6. faith in ourselves to will the truth, 7. freedom from resentment under persecution, 8. freedom from resentment under wrong, 9. ability to distinguish right from wrong, and 10. ability to distinguish the real from the unreal.

These virtues were taught to African students and eventually taught to the Greeks that valued this education to the degree that they risked persecution by studying in Egypt. In this institution students often entered at the age of seven and did not graduate until they were forty-seven years of age. The Grand Lodge of Wa'at was not just concerned about the transmission of knowledge but they were concerned about the development of character. They were also concerned about the development of a value system that would produce the kind of scholar that would be committed to these virtues. In the last chapter we will look at what happens when we do not have these types of institutions to develop this type of character, we will have schools that will produce African scholars like Clarence Thomas who have little to no commitment to the liberation struggle. In the Grand Lodge of Wa'at, via these virtues, they felt that it was not enough to have a B.A., M.A., and Ph.D., and not have a value system that was commensurate with the laws of MAAT and the Nguzo Saba.

Another conversion model which has its roots in Africa is the "Rites of Passage." Paul Hill has written an outstanding book entitled, *Coming of Age: African American Male Rites of Passage*. In the book which is applicable to both males and females, Paul Hill mentions the minimal standards of rites of passage that all the youth should go through. They should develop an understanding of spirituality, African American history and culture, Nguzo Saba, cooperative economics, community service, the importance physical development, government, leadership, and affluency in a foreign language. Paul Hill also mentions the ten basic principles of African education that we desperately need here in America. They are as follows: 1. separating the child from the community and routines of daily life, 2. observing nature, 3. a social process based on age, 4. rejection of childhood, 5. listening to elders, 6. purification rituals, 7. test of character, 8. use of special language, 9. use of a special name, and 10. symbolic resurrection.[13]

Africans in the diaspora need to draw upon the rich history and culture from continental Africa and implement these into our homes, schools, churches, community organizations, and most importantly in rites of passage programs that can convert the Hip-Hop and New Jack generation. We mentioned earlier that values require a foundation and we cited that the best foundation is a relationship with God. One of the major value crisis among our youth and many adults is the lack of moral teaching, spiritual values, and ethical nourishment that everyone needs in order to make the proper decisions. There has never been a dearth of spiritual wisdom in the African community. Under the scholarship of Yosef ben-Jochannan in the book titled, *African Origins of the Major Western Religions,* it documents that the origins of Judaism, Christianity, and Islam all have their roots in Africa.

The Osirian drama or the weighing of the heart in the Scales of Thoth describe the day of judgment. Listed below are some of the 147 Negative Confessions that were developed approximately 2527 B.C. These 147 Negative Confessions, also classified as the "Declarations of Innocence" precede Moses, another African born in Egypt around 1300 B.C. He was also inspired by the Holy Spirit to give us the Ten Commandments. Notice how closely the "Declarations of Innocence" parallel the Ten Commandments.

1) I have done violence to no man.
2) I have not committed theft.
3) I have not uttered falsehood.
4) I have not uttered evil words.
5) I have not defiled the wife of a man.
6) I have not violated sacred times and seasons.
7) I have not cursed God.

Moses on Mt. Sinai, approximately 1250 B.C. gave us the following:

1) Thou shalt have no other God before me.
2) Thou shalt not bow down to any idol of worship.
3) Do not make for yourselves images of anything in heaven or on earth.
4) Observe the Sabbath and keep it holy.
5) Respect your father and your mother.
6) Do not commit murder.
7) Do not commit adultery.
8) Do not steal.
9) Do not accuse anyone falsely.
10) Do not desire another man's wife.[14]

Unfortunately, many of our youth have not been taught spiritual laws. Many Christians have not been taught that Moses was an African and that preceding Moses there were other Africans who had developed laws of morality. In the religion of Islam, the word Muslim means one who has become peaceful and submits to the will of God. There are five pillars of Islam. The first pillar is the belief in one God. The second pillar is to pray at least five times per day. The third pillar is the commandment that you should sacrifice a part of your wealth to God. The fourth pillar is fasting especially in the month of Ramadan. The fifth pillar is the pilgrimage to Mecca. People that have not been raised on spiritual laws or commandments, who have not been taught the power of prayer underestimate its impact on the present values in America. In the book titled, *America: To Pray or Not to Pray* by David Barton, he documents quantitatively the impact that the absence of prayer and spiritual laws have had on America.

The most significant year was 1962. It was in the school year of 1962 through 1963 that 39 million students and over two million teachers were barred from praying in school. Prayer is the quintessential religious practice. Prayer is an acknowledgment of God. It is the simplest identification of a philosophy which recognizes God and His laws and standards of conduct. Prayer being the heart of religion was the first target of an atheist minority and a lackadaisical Christian following. The prayer that had been allowed to be shared in school was as follows: Almighty God, we acknowledge our dependence upon thee, and we beg thy blessing upon us, our parents, our teachers, and our country. After the removal of prayer, there soon followed cases rejecting the Bible and any values derived from them such as the Ten Commandments, the teaching of premarital sexual abstinence to students, etc. Prayer, like values, requires a foundation, the foundation being a relationship to God. The following charts illustrate what took place in America immediately after 1962, once prayer was taken out of schools.[15]

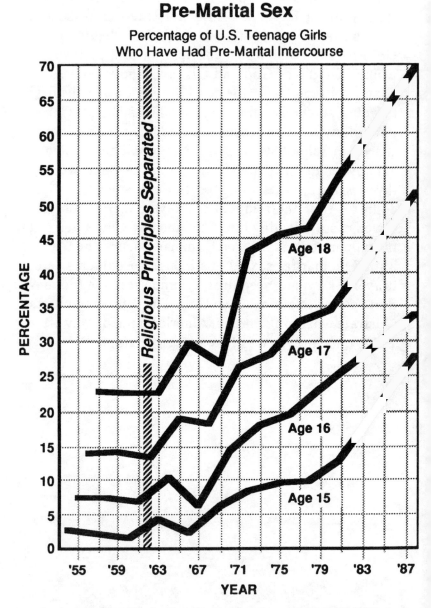

Pre-Marital Sex

Percentage of U.S. Teenage Girls
Who Have Had Pre-Marital Intercourse

Religious Principles Separated

Age 18

Age 17

Age 16

Age 15

PERCENTAGE

YEAR

Basic data from *Family Planning Perspectives*, March/April 1987, and from *Sexual and Reproductive Behavior of American Women, 1982-88*. Furnished by the Alan Guttmacher Institute.

Pregnancies To Unwed Girls
15-19 Years Of Age

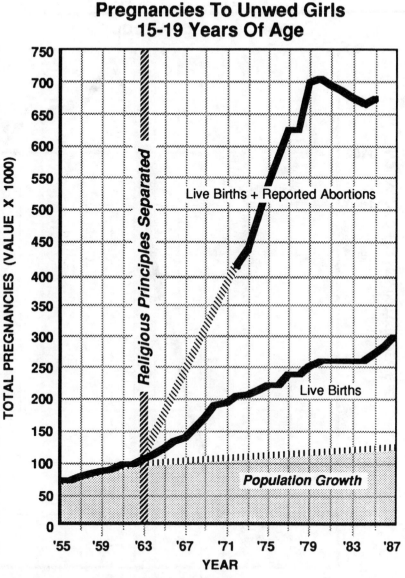

IIIIIIIIIIIII Indicates population growth.
〰〰〰〰〰〰 Indicates interpolated data.

Basic data from Department of Health and Human Services,
Statistical Abstracts of the United States, the Center for Disease Control,
and the Department of Commerce, Census Bureau.

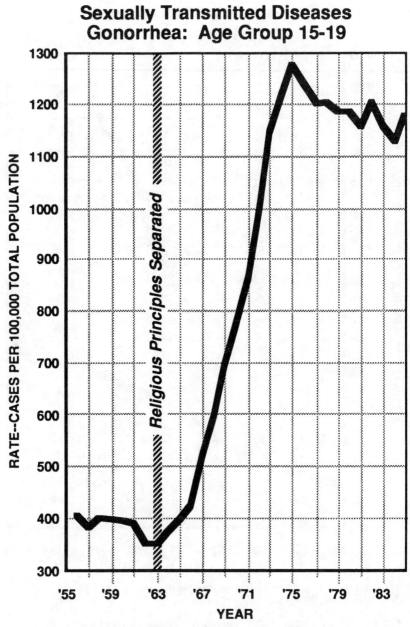

Sexually Transmitted Diseases
Gonorrhea: Age Group 15-19

RATE--CASES PER 100,000 TOTAL POPULATION

Religious Principles Separated

YEAR

Basic data from the Center for Disease Control and
Department of Health and Human Resources.

Divorce Rates

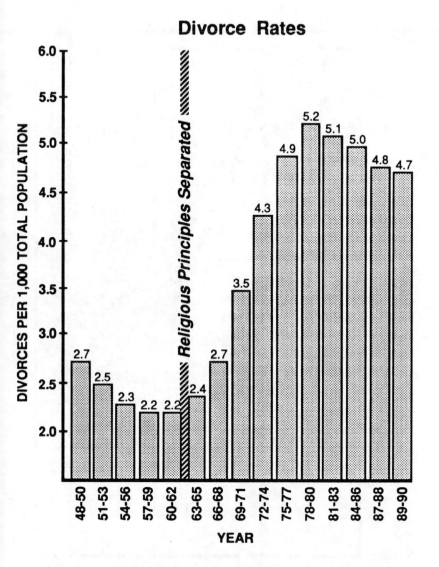

"The U.S. is at the top of the world's divorce charts on marital breakups.
U.S. News and World Report, June 8, 1987, pp. 68-69.

"The number of divorces tripled each year between 1962 and 1981."
Time, July 13, 1987, p. 21.

Basic data from the U. S. National Center for Health Statistics,
Vital Statistics of the United States, annual.

SAT Total Scores

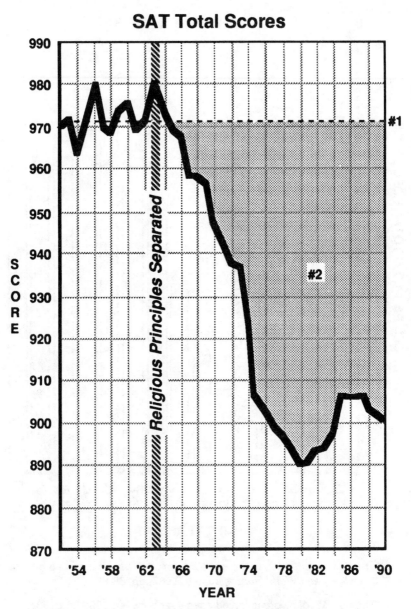

#1 - Average achievement level prior to the separation

#2 - Amount of reduced academic achievement since the separation

Basic data from the College Entrance Exam Board.

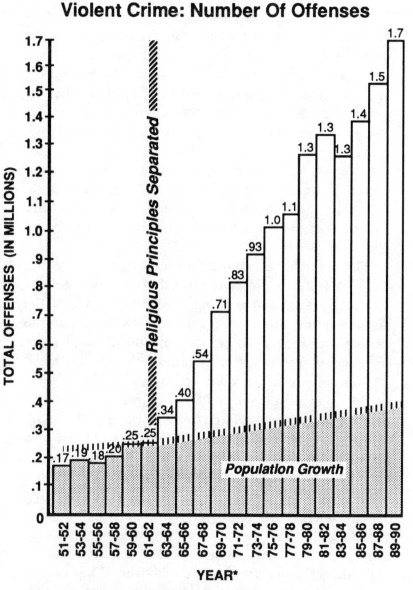

Violent Crime: Number Of Offenses

TOTAL OFFENSES (IN MILLIONS)

1.7
1.6
1.5
1.4
1.3
1.2
1.1
1.0
.9
.8
.7
.6
.5
.4
.3
.2
.1
0

Religious Principles Separated

.17 .19 .18 .20 .25 .25 .34 .40 .54 .71 .83 .93 1.0 1.1 1.3 1.3 1.3 1.4 1.5 1.7

Population Growth

YEAR*

51-52 53-54 55-56 57-58 59-60 61-62 63-64 65-66 67-68 69-70 71-72 73-74 75-76 77-78 79-80 81-82 83-84 85-86 87-88 89-90

IIIIIIIIII Indicates population growth profile.

* Groupings represent average rate per year over the two-year period.

Basic data from *Statistical Abstracts of the United States,*
and the Department of Commerce, Census Bureau.

One of the fundamental problems that has happened with America over the past 30 plus years is that monies allocated toward sex education do not include the fundamental position of abstinence. Sex outside of marriage is fornication and is a sin. Unfortunately, because America no longer teaches the values of abstinence, then this trend will continue to increase. In our concluding chapter, one of the issues that we will look at is the decision on whether someone should marry or live together. If there are no rules, if there are no values, if there is no relationship to God, then people will make their individual decisions because they are not required to adhere to higher principles, morals and ethics.

The second chart shows the increase in divorce that also illustrates a direct relationship between the absence of prayer and a rising divorce rate. While the divorce rate is one of every three in 18 months in the secular world, it becomes one of 244 if couples are saved, pray, read scripture and attend church together.[16]

The third chart I want to review is the one on academic achievement and SAT scores. America had been on the rise as it related to SAT scores, until 1962. As soon as prayer was taken out of schools there was a significant decline in SAT scores. The minimal increase that you see on the chart is more of a reflection of an increasing number of children that are attending private schools where prayer is still allowed.

The last chart I want to review is the one on violent crimes and that too has increased as prayer, morality and values are seldom taught to children. When are we going to realize that there is power in prayer and that Africans long ago realized that every one must submit to God? There were laws, values and ethics, whether we call them the Negative Confessions, Declarations of Innocence or the Ten Commandments. If allowed to act without a value system that is not connected to a relationship to God then our present social ills will continue. This present Hip-Hop, New Jack generation needs a value system that is pro-God, life, liberation, and respectful of women and elders. They need a value system that's cooperative, collective, and with the accent on internal development. This value system is available to us spiritually, historically and culturally through religion, MAAT, and the Nguzo Saba.

There are many virtues that are attributed to MAAT. The most frequent are righteousness, truth, justice, order, harmony, reciprocity, and balance. MAAT is symbolized by a feather. It is present in the weighing process as each individual on judgement day is evaluated on these cardinal virtues mentioned above. In the Husia, Maulana Karenga describes some of the various virtues of MAAT. ''I have done what the people love and God praises. I was one truly venerated and had no faults. Who gave bread to the hungry and clothes to the naked. I put an end to pain and erased wrong doing. I supported the aged, and satisfied the have nots. I was a shelter for the child and help to the widow. One who gave rank even to an infant. I did these things knowing their value and knowing their reward from the Lord of MAAT.''

''I kept my mouth free from attacking those who attacked me. My patience turned my foes into friends and my enemies into allies. I was one who spoke justly, who repeated that which was pleasing to hear. When the messenger of death comes to take you let him find you ready to go to your resting place saying, 'Here comes one prepared before you'. Not arrogant because of your knowledge. Take council with the ignorant as well as with the wise. Be diligent as long as you live. Always doing more than is commanded of you. If you are a leader be courteous and listen carefully to the presentations of partitioners. Not all that is asked for can be granted but a fair hearing satisfies the heart. If you wish your conduct to be perfect, to be free from all that is evil, guard against the vice of greed for material things. Share with our friends that which you have for that which is yours is a gift of God. May your spirit be always kind, may you always forgive.''[17]

In order for us to believe in the virtues of MAAT we have to believe that we are going to be judged by our maker. A book could be written on each of the principles of MAAT, but the two that I think are most significant are righteousness and harmony. Molefi Asante says that one cannot be righteous alone. It is a continuous process by which we align ourselves with the harmony we find in nature. Thus righteousness is a process and when we say ''be righteous'' we mean for the moment in that particular context. Through the laws of MAAT, we must ask ourselves in every situation are we righteous?

Can we love God, believe in MAAT and the Nguzo Saba and list 37 reasons why we would kill somebody? People that make these decisions suffer from a lack of values and a foundation in which to be anchored. We have come a long way from ancient Egypt (Kemet). I believe in the heart of every gang banger, drug dealer, fornicator, adulterer, and sinner (which we all are) is righteousness. There is harmony in man and nature. There is both good and evil and the Lord gives us a choice. Good exceeds evil and in the law of MAAT where there is evil, the Lord will provide righteousness.

Our community needs healing. Many youth and adults lack a relationship with God and lack a value system like MAAT. Those within our community that are striving toward righteousness, truth, justice, order, harmony, reciprocity and balance need to share that with the Hip-Hop, New Jack generation. The more contemporary value system, the Nguzo Saba that we also want to share in this chapter was developed by Maulana Karenga in 1966. It originates from the ideology of Kawaida which means tradition and reason. The Nguzo Saba is an attempt to draw upon our African past which includes MAAT and interject that into the 21st century America. Listed below are the seven principles of the Nguzo Saba which coincide with the seven days of Kwanzaa where each day has a principle.

1) Umoja - (unity)
2) Kujichagulia - (self-determination)
3) Ujima - (collective work and responsibility)
4) Ujamaa - (cooperative economics)
5) Nia - (purpose)
6) Kuumba - (creativity)
7) Imani - (faith)

In Chapter One where we were looking at vignettes, one of the short stories that I told was where I was around a group of African Americans who understood the Nguzo Saba theoretically, but in its actual practice was not motivated to even ask if I wanted something to drink or something to eat. I am very concerned about people memorizing a set of values but not practicing them. I've been at conferences where conscious African Americans have played "Blacker than Thou" games with each other. They have an African name, dress in African attire, and pronounce all Kiswahili words, and argue for days at a conference on whether the word should be Afrocentricity or Africentricity. There are people who call themselves leaders who can't forgive and keep internal feuds going far beyond people's memories. Our people will be more inclined to follow us if they see our value system is able to transform differences and allow people to work together in harmony versus whose read the most books and how many times they've visited Africa.

I have tried to make the Nguzo Saba more concrete and less theoretical and perfunctory. When I hear the word Umoja (Unity), I think of the concept operational unity. Linda Myers in her book, *Optimal Psychology*, poses we should not look for differences but similarities. I'm asking all nationalists, Christians, Muslims, Hip-Hop, and New Jack followers to put aside our differences and look for commonalities. I once heard a story where 100 Whites were meeting and disagreed on 99 issues, but concluded the meeting united on the major issue. Across town, 100 African Americans were also meeting and agreed on 99 points, but because they couldn't resolve the last issue concluded the meeting with dissension.

The second principle is Kujichagulia - (self-determination). To make this value come alive I think of the word "can't." If you believe in this principle you will never use this word again and you'll improve your endurance and tenacity. The third principle is Ujima - (collective work and responsibility). It means that whenever you're visiting someone you will offer assistance and even if they decline you will do something. We must treat our neighbor's home like our own.

The fourth principle is Ujamaa - (cooperative economics). It means that you will identify African American businesses and support them. You will also make a notation in your checkbook of the number of African American businesses versus non-African American businesses that you support. The fifth principle is Nia - (purpose). It means that you will join at least one organization and operate under the principle of 110 which requires striving for excellence. The sixth principle is Kuumba - (creativity). It means that you will never litter anymore in your neighborhood and you will do whatever you can to enhance your wardrobe, home and neighborhood. The seventh principle is Imani - (faith). It means that you will have a personal relationship with God which requires prayer and the reading of scripture. Let's now apply these values to contemporary issues in the following chapter.

Clarence Thomas is an example of the American value system which perpetuates individualism, competition, and materialism.

CHAPTER FOUR

From Nehemiah to Clarence

"The Lord asked Cain, 'Where is your brother Abel?' I don't know. Am I supposed to take care of my brother?" Genesis 4:9

"It has always annoyed me to hear from the mouths of certain arbiters of Blackness that middle class Blacks should reach back and pull up those Blacks less fortunate than they." Shelby Steele, *The Content of our Character*

"Then I heard the Lord say, 'Whom shall I send? Who will be our messenger?' I answered, I will go. Send me." Isaiah 6:8

"To whom much is given, much is also required." Luke 12:48

I believe that Clarence Thomas, Shelby Steele and youth that represent the New Jack generation share the same value system. For this reason, I believe they are dangerous. It becomes obvious when we have youth that will kill you because you looked at them the wrong way, talked to their lady, had your cap on the wrong side, or it was the wrong color. It's obvious that these people suffer from a lack of positive values. The value system of Hip-Hop and New Jack is individualistic, competitive and very materialistic.

Drug dealers sell death to their community. Drugs that can potentially be consumed by their own family members. They have no regard for the consequences because their primary value is money. Let us not be confused that the same value system of New Jack resides within most Fortune 500 executives, Trilateral Commissioners, Mafia, and Negroes like Clarence Thomas, who after disrespecting Anita Hill during the years they worked together, one of his first decisions on the Supreme Court was to take away any rights that an inmate would have and give complete authority to prison officials. I chose Clarence Thomas because he is the role model that the establishment projects to African Americans. It is imperative in a capitalistic society where there will be more losers than winners that you create the illusion that everyone can be rich. The most effective way of doing that is to show individuals, regardless of how small a percentage, those who have been able to overcome their meager origins. The media loves to compare immigrants to slaves to reinforce the idea that anyone can make it in America and that the United States is still the ''melting pot'' of the world. The fallacy of this argument is that you do not compare someone that voluntarily came here to a group that was forced via slavery. You don't compare a group that brought their culture, education and economic resources with them to a group denied their culture, where reading was a criminal offense, and never paid for the labor they provided between 1619 and 1865, which the committee for reparations has calculated is 4.1 trillion dollars plus inflation and interest.

The virtue of hard work does not belong to the Fortune 500, the Trilateral Commission and the Republican Party. It is a virtue that Africans have always possessed. Had we been a lazy people there would have been no reason to bring us to America in the first place. Ironically, if the oppressor had such a strong work ethic they should have used themselves as their servants. The same value system that is possessed by someone who would sell drugs to his people is the same value system of the mafia and drug lords that have created a drug industry where 76% of the users are now White.

A major concern with Clarence Thomas is unlike Paul Robeson, Clarence Thomas believes Shelby Steele when he says, ''I got mine and you got yours to get.'' He believes he made it solely via hard work and the ''bootstrap theory,'' and that he has no responsibility to give time and resources back to a community that is suffering. Paul Robeson in his moment of glory rather than accepting all the accolades chose to indict a system that was unfair to the masses of people. Not only did Robeson choose to indict the process, but he also gave of himself to a depressed community. Many people that possess the value system of Clarence Thomas are unable to imagine that they possess the same values as New Jack, the Mafia and the Trilateral Commission.

I remember having a conversation with Robert Woodson from the National Center for Neighborhood Enterprise and he was sharing with me that he had grown leery of the civil rights struggle when he observed the results of a successful march and protest to achieve a greater number of employees at a particular company in West Virginia, only to find that they were only going to hire professionals. In this case approximately eight to nine engineers, who when interviewed within a course of a year said that they got the job because of their qualifications and it had nothing to do with the pressure that the civil rights advocates had brought to bear. The major concern that we had with this scenario is that those engineers represent the kind of values that Clarence Thomas possess, but more importantly, the ultimate objective hopefully of the civil rights era was to empower the ''least of these.'' That has not been the case if we review the statistics over the past 25-30 years.

Manning Marable points out, "First desegregation did not benefit the entire black community uniformly. Black professionals and managers, those who had attended colleges and technical schools, were the principal beneficiaries. Working class African Americans also benefitted from income increases as new opportunities were created in upper income levels of a labor force; their children for the first time had access to higher education but opportunity in a capitalist society is always a function of social class position, which means ownership of capital, material resources, education and access to power. For the unemployed, the poor and those without marketable skills or resources, for those whose lives were circumscribed by illiteracy, disease and desperation "race" continued to be a central factor in their marginal existence."[1]

Numerous studies point out that these civil rights, social welfare pimps design programs for the poor and yet if you look at their budget, 80% of the economic resources go to these "New Jack- Clarence Thomas's" and only twenty percent go to the people supposedly they were designed to serve. These same political pimps then in private conversations and sometimes in public to the people that they serve indict them for possessing a negative value system. In the outstanding book by Brenda Wall on the *Rodney King Rebellion*, she points out that if we do not understand the values of empowerment, liberation, MAAT, the Nguzo Saba, we will make the mistake of simply thinking that dropping money into South Central LA by people who possess a Hip-Hop, New Jack, Clarence Thomas, Fortune 500, Mafia, Bloods, Crips and Trilateral Commission value system is not going to be productive. We need Africans like Nehemiah who had heard that the walls of Jerusalem had been torn down and felt it was his responsibility to return home and rebuild the wall.

I never will forget how the book of Nehemiah became so vivid for me. I was speaking in Newark, NJ and a very close friend of mine had shared with me that she was taught to secure the best education she could and then move as soon as she could out of Newark into suburbia. It was only after reading the book of Nehemiah that she felt compelled to return home and rebuild her wall. There is a mammoth amount of rebuilding needed in the South Centrals nationwide. One-third of all African Americans and one-half of all children live below the poverty line. The median income for African Americans over the past 25 years has only fluctuated between 57% and 61% of White income. It's ironic how close this is to being three-fifths of a person.

Before we analyze what Nehemiah and African Americans who believe in the principles of MAAT and Nguzo Saba must do with that portion of our community that represent the least of these, we need to better understand how statistics are used. While we are not pleased that one-third of all African Americans live below the poverty line, the juxtaposition is two-thirds are living above the poverty line. Unfortunately, the media does not show them as much as they portray the one-third. You would presume that all African Americans are poor. You would also assume that the majority of the people that are living below the poverty line are African American. There are 35.5 million Americans living below the poverty line, 5.4 are Hispanic, 9.3 are African American, and 20.8 are White. For some reason the media has no problem finding the 9.3 million African Americans that live below the poverty line, but they seem to have difficulty finding the 20.8 million White Americans that are also living below the poverty line.[2]

The obvious reason of course is racism, but the

other reason could be that with the 20.8 million Whites that are living below the poverty line are in scattered site housing and rural areas. Unfortunately, the 9.3 million African Americans have all been placed on top of each other in ''projects'' which research studies have always documented is not the best way to house people nor rats. While we acknowledge that one-third of our race lives below the poverty line, we need to also mention that 25% of our race has an income that exceeds $40,000. It should also be pointed out that while one half of all African American children live below the poverty line, that does not translate to one-half of all families because middle income families have fewer children. Researchers have also found that when we hold income constant then the values of hard work, savings and education are persistent in the White and Black communities. At the same time, while it is important to point out some of the class distinctions within our race, we need to also document that values transcend income. The superior work of Reginald Clark in the book titled, *Family Life and School Achievement* looked at low income, middle income, and single and two parent homes and found that the major factor was not income nor the number of parents, but values and the quality of the interaction. Low income, single parents could and do produce high achieving students. The best example of that is Benjamin Carson, who was failing fourth grade, born in a low income family to a single parent mother who only had a seventh grade education. Just as the Lord had His Son born in a barn, one of the best neurosurgeons in the country grew up from those modest beginnings.

Julius Wilson points out in the book, *Truly Disadvantaged,* ''The culture of poverty has both an adaptation and a reaction of the poor to their marginal position in a class stratified highly individual capitalistic society.." He also points out "this cultural poverty comes into existence. It tends to perpetuate itself from generation to generation because of its affect on the children by the time slum children are age six or seven they have usually absorbed the basic values and attitudes of their subculture and are not psychologically geared to take full advantage of changing conditions or increased opportunities which may occur in their lifetime."[3]

It has always been a debate on the relationship between income and values, between opportunity and values. An example of how values are reflected as it relates to income concerning teenage pregnancy. Kenneth Clark has argued, "In the ghetto, the meaning of the illegitimate child is not ultimate disgrace. There is not the demand for abortion or for surrender of the child that one finds in more privileged communities. In the middle class community the disgrace of illegitimacy is tied to personal and family aspirations. In lower class families, on the other hand the girl loses only some of her already limited options by having an illegitimate child. She is not going to make a "better marriage" or improve her economic and social status either way. On the contrary, a child is a symbol of the fact that she is a woman, and she may gain from having something of her own. Nor is the boy who fathers an illegitimate child going to lose, for where is he going? The path to any higher status seems closed to him in any case."[4]

In our conclusion, we're going to analyze the issue of abortion and marriage versus living together within the context of values in more detail. This chapter is an attempt to remind the reader that the alien value system possessed by Hip-Hop and New Jack also resides in African Americans like Clarence Thomas and other

119

members of the "middle class." The disdain that Shelby Steele and others possess resenting having to give back to the community comes from the larger value system of America. In numerous books: *Two Nations* by Andrew Hacker, *The Minority Party* by Peter Brown, *Race* by Studs Terkel, they all point out that America is increasingly becoming two separate and unequal societies. It was a separate society during slavery, in 1896 with Plessy versus Ferguson, in 1968 when the National Advisory Commission on civil disorders pointed out "our nation is moving toward two societies. One black, one white, separate and unequal."

Andrew Hacker points out in the book that many Whites have the same values as Shelby Steele with regards to their role in trying to equalize the two societies. "If white Americans regard the United States as their nation they also see it with racial problems they feel are not of their making. Some contrast current conditions with earlier times, when blacks appeared more willing to accept a subordinate status. Most whites will protest that they bear neither the responsibility nor blame for the conditions blacks face. Neither they or their forbearers ever owned slaves, nor can they see themselves as having held anyone back or down. Most white Americans believe that for at least the last generation blacks have been given more than a fair chance and at least equal opportunity, if not outright advantages. Moreover, few white Americans feel obliged to ponder how membership in the major race gives them power and privileges."[5]

Peter Brown reinforces this notion in his book *Minority Party* where he writes that many Whites feel that the democratic party is the party for poor people and minorities. Brown points out that in Macomb County in Michigan in 1960 two-thirds of the White

120

population there voted democratic for John F. Kennedy. In 1980 that same population voted for Ronald Reagan, a Republican. His analysis is that Whites in the 1960s felt guilt and some level of responsibility for the level of discrimination. He documents that in 1980 Whites no longer felt that way and that whatever debt that they needed to pay was paid with the signing of the civil rights act by Lyndon Johnson in 1964.[6]

I could write another book on the psychology of racism and as Bobby Wright pointed out that racist Whites possess what he called a ''psychopathic racial personality.'' Somehow they believe that 244 years of free labor can be repaid with a civil rights act being signed in 1964. Jonathan Kozol is another writer that points out how wide the gap has become in these two societies in the excellent book titled, *Savage Inequalities*. While America is a nation that provides public school education for everyone due to the fact that it is based on the property tax and because of the tremendous segregation in the society, studies indicate that there are very few integrated neighborhoods and that the threshold seems to be an eight percent Black population.[7]

When the population exceeds this figure there seems to be an increase in ''White flight.'' Because public school education is based on the property tax that means that those neighborhoods where there is a higher median income and real estate value those school districts will allocate a larger amount per pupil. While theoretically states are charged with the responsibility of providing the additional funds so that school districts will pretty much operate equally, that is not the case. In my home state Illinois alone, there are school districts like Ford Heights and East St. Louis that allocate between $2,500 - $3,500 per student and there are other school districts like Nile Township and New Trier near $14,000. Listed below are tables in the 88-89 school year for the states of Illinois, New Jersey and New York which if you consider present year figures makes the gap even more significant.

TABLE I

School Funding in the Chicago Area
(Figures for the 1988–1989 School Year)

School or District	Spending Per Pupil
Niles Township High School	$9,371
New Trier High School	$8,823
Glencoe (elementary and junior high schools)	$7,363
Winnetka (elementary and junior high schools)	$7,059
Wilmette (elementary and junior high schools)	$6,009
Chicago (average of all grade levels)	$5,265

SOURCE: Chicago Panel on School Policy and Finance.

TABLE II

School Funding in New Jersey
(Figures for the 1988–1989 School Year)

District	Spending Per Pupil
Princeton	$7,725
Summit	$7,275
West Orange	$6,505
Cherry Hill	$5,981
Jersey City	$4,566
East Orange	$4,457
Paterson	$4,422
Camden	$3,538

SOURCE: Educational Law Center, Newark, New Jersey.

TABLE III

School Funding in the New York City Area
(Figures for the 1986–1987 School Year)

District	Spending Per Pupil
Manhasset	$11,372
Jericho	$11,325
Great Neck	$11,265
Bronxville	$10,113
Rye	$9,092
Yonkers	$7,399
Levittown	$6,899
Mount Vernon	$6,433
Roosevelt	$6,339
New York City	$5,585

SOURCE: "Statistical Profiles of School Districts" (New York State Board of Education).

TABLE IV

The Widening Gap
(School Funding in Six Districts in the New York City Area: Changes in a Three-Year Period)

District	1986–1987 School Year	1989–1990 School Year
Manhasset	$11,372	$15,084
Jericho	$11,325	$14,355
Great Neck	$11,265	$15,594
Mount Vernon	$6,433	$9,112
Roosevelt	$6,339	$8,349
New York City	$5,585	$7,299

SOURCES: "Statistical Profiles of School Districts" (New York State Board of Education) and New York Times.

As Ron Edmond said as it related to education, "We know all that we need to know to teach all children." America has enough resources where no one has to go to sleep, hungry or homeless. It is not a question of resources. It is a question of values. Gail Inlow points out that the principle is that our culture places a higher value on materialism than it does on humanism. While paying lip service to the 'good life for all' concept, it refuses to pay the cost to bring it about.[9] There are numerous problems with our school system. We've pointed out throughout this book that two of the major problems are 1) when prayer was removed from school 1962 and the immediate decline in SAT scores and 2) the unequitable distribution of funding between low income school districts and higher income school districts. Both of these reflect the values of our society.

There is a third major factor where values are portrayed - tracking. This is a concept where you divide children into groups based on their abilities. The concept uses many names; advanced placement, honors, regular, basic, gifted and talented, special ed, and magnet schools, but it all means the same. You're dividing children based on ability. All studies indicate that those in the lowest tracks seldom catch those in the highest tracks. Studies by Asa Hilliard, Barbara Sizemore, John Goodlad, Jonathan Kozol, Jeannie Oakes, Ray Rist, and myself all point out that tracking is not effective for all children. It is beneficial for a few children and is easier for teachers, but it is not the best system for all children.

The question we need to ask ourselves is why is tracking maintained? The answer lies in our values. The economy does not need every student to graduate with a B.A., M.A. and Ph.D. The economy needs winners and losers, and that is what schools produce.

Businesses need a portion of the population that will work for McDonald's, clean hotels and all other forms of menial labor, and they need another segment of the population that will become its engineers, computer programmers and its overall brain trust. The decision to maintain tracking is a value decision. It is a decision made by the economy and reinforced by schools.

Numerous studies point out that when we have mixed ability groups then those students that are higher achievers will have the opportunity to help the lower achievers and that will improve their skills. This is one of the major strengths of cooperative learning. Clarence Thomas and New Jacks are no accidents. They are a perfect example of school systems where children seldom if ever are encouraged to help the "least of these." How can we expect Hip-Hop, New Jack, Clarence Thomas, or Shelby Steele not to feel the need to volunteer in the African American community when they were never encouraged in school? It is very possible to go K-8, 9-12 and college and never be asked by your teacher to help your peers. Schools teach more than academics - they teach values.

A friend of mine in Milwaukee calls this "the design purpose machine." Schools like other machines have a purpose. The purpose of schools is either to destroy you or to have you to graduate with a value system that is Eurocentric, individualistic, competitive and materialistic. Most of us would acknowledge that the school system has failed large numbers of African American children as reflected in a drop-out rate that in many cities exceeds 50% and where 42% of African American youth, 17 years of age can't read beyond a sixth grade reading level; and 41% of the children placed in special education are African American. The second premise of this design purpose machine is that if you do not come out of the school system destroyed you come out more committed to the red, white and blue, IBM, the Bloods and the Crips than you do to the red, black and green and the liberation of your people. The question we need to ask ourselves is how do you defeat a design purpose machine. The first issue you need to do is to become more aware by reading additional books and developing your value system from New Jack and Hip-Hop to MAAT and the Nguzo Saba. Once you become aware, then you have filters so when you're in school you can decipher the truth from the lies. Third, to begin to act like a foreigner with the attitude of taking in as much as you possibly can with the objective being like my friend in Newark and Nehemiah, to return home and rebuild the wall. We have said throughout this book that values require a foundation. I believe the best foundation is a relationship to God. We have to raise the questions to New Jack, Hip-Hop, Clarence Thomas, and Shelby Steele that were raised in Matthew 25:35-40: "When I was hungry, did you feed me? When I was thirsty, did you give me a drink? When I was a stranger, did you receive me in your home? When I was naked, did you clothe me? When I was sick, did you take care of me? When I was in prison, did you visit me?" The unrighteous will then answer Him, "When Lord did we ever see you hungry and feed you or when you were thirsty, did we give you a drink? When did we ever see you a stranger and welcome you in our homes or naked and clothed you? When did we ever see you sick or in prison and visit you?" The King will reply, "I tell you whenever you did this for one of the least important of these brothers of mine you did it for me."

There are many "vertical christians" who say they love the Lord that they have not seen but can't reach out for their brothers and sisters that they see each and every day. There is something wrong with their value system. John Perkins in, *With Justice For All* points out that there are three major principles for community development. They include relocation, reconciliation and redistribution. John states, "I noticed how Jesus approached the woman. He came to her on her territory. He chose to go through Samaria. Jews traveling from Judea to Galilee usually crossed over the Jordan river and went around Samaria because of their prejudice. A Jew meeting a Samaritan on the road would cross to the other side to keep even the shadow of a Samaritan from touching him. Jesus deliberately went through Samaria for one reason--He wanted to personally touch the lives of the people there (relocation). Secondly, the Holy Spirit showed me this profound truth: Jesus's love and his bodily presence in a community could reconcile people."

"God commands us to love and to forgive one another. Our love for one another demonstrates to the world that we are indeed disciples (reconciliation). Third, I saw how Jesus opened the conversation with the woman. He let her determine the starting point of the conversation. She was at the well to get water; He asked for a drink. Notice that He didn't just talk about her need; He brought his own need. Her need was water; His need was water and by asking her to help Him he affirmed her dignity. Man's most deeply felt need is to have his dignity affirmed. He wants to feel his somebodyness-to know that he is a person of worth. That is what the woman at the well needed to know. She needed to know that she was as good as a Jew."[10]

Christ calls us to share with those in need. This calls for redistributing more than our goods. It means sharing our skills, our time, our energy, and our gospel in ways that empower people to break out of this cycle of poverty and assume responsibility for their own needs (redistribution). We need Clarence Thomas, Shelby Steele, New Jacks, and the Hip-Hop generation to become actively involved in the following empowerment programs:

1) Afterschool and Cultural awareness programs

2) Tutorial and Test-taking programs

3) Scholarships

4) Role model programs

5) Rites of Passage programs

6) Monitoring liquor and cigarette billboard advertisements

7) Ujamaa (developing entrepreneurs)

8) Community of Men (a crime watch organization)

Let's now move to the conclusion and summarize the relationship between values and some of the fundamental issues that values impact such as abortion, marriage, welfare, gun control, and ultimately, acculturation.

Parents must instill strong, positive values within their children at an early age.

CONCLUSION

Drugs, crime, unemployment, poverty, miseducation, and teen-age pregnancy are symptoms of our three major problems-racism, lack of self-knowledge, and values.
--Jawanza Kunjufu

There has been an increasing debate in this country as it relates to values, and the relationship between values and premarital sex, marriage versus living together, abortion, welfare, gun control, and the legalization of drugs. In the third chapter, I pointed out that when prayer was taken out of school numerous indicators rose and one of them was premarital sex. By the age of 18, 70% are sexually active. Premarital sexual activity among 15-year-old students has increased almost 500% with half of sexually active males having had their first sexual experience between the ages of 11 and 13. Sexually transmitted diseases i.e., gonorrhea and syphilis have increased over 200% and teenage pregnancies have increased over 400% causing the United States to become the Western leader in teenage pregnancy with 1.25 million adolescent pregnancies each year. African American females lead the world in teen pregnancy followed by Arabs, and White Americans.

What many people may not be aware of is that while it is important that children are given information about human sexuality, it is also important to know that of the students who have gone through a comprehensive sex education program, 65% of them are sexually active. This percentage is almost twice the size as those who have not completed a sex education curriculum. Additionally 42% of those who have never been in a comprehensive sex education class which promotes promiscuous intercourse of the sexes have not had sexual intercourse.[1] I'm in full agreement that young people need to be taught sex education, but sex education without values and a relationship to God is not a comprehensive sex education program. The statistics appear to show that the sex education programs encourage sexual activity, instead of teaching abstinence.

Remember, it was not long ago that "Magic" initially even having the AIDS virus went through the same propaganda that most of these sex education programs offer- and that was "safe sex"- whatever that is in the 1990s. Only after being challenged numerous times, did he acquiesce. My first suggestion is to abstain, but that seems to be a word that most adults cannot say to youth. The tremendous influx of rap records that promote sexual activity, videos that describe it in graphic detail, and advertisements supposedly promoting a car or soap but use sex, make it difficult for our youth. Their brain computers simply have not been programmed with any information that give them the understanding that sex and marriage are synonymous.

The Family Institute On Values points out that this behavior reflects a widespread change in values: in 1967, 85% of Americans condemned premarital sex as morally wrong, compared to only 37% in 1979. The sexual revolution has been a major contributor to a striking increase in unwed parenthood. Non-marital births jumped from five percent of all births in 1960 (22% of black births) to 22% in 1985 (60% of black births).[2] Unfortunately, many people still believe that they do what they want to do and that no one made the decision but them. It is only when you look at things from a historical perspective, that you begin to understand the impact of the media, and understand the relationship that God, prayer and values, or the lack of it can have on your life. This first issue premarital sex is just the tip of the iceberg as it reflects America's values.

I mentioned in the introduction that this will be one of the most challenging books I've ever written because all of my books are written with the objective of hoping I can somehow influence and change behavior. I understand that values run very deep and that they are the driving force for behavior and that values are taught very early and unfortunately, taught by institutions and people that are not influenced by God, MAAT, and the Nguzo Saba, In this conclusionary chapter, my first objective is to recommend that sex education classes teach abstinence. Sex education programs are not comprehensive if it only includes biology and media, and does not include God, MAAT and the Nguzo Saba. There has been a debate surrounding many high schools having clinics within their facilities which many people call ''condom distribution centers.'' Schools acknowledge that they do perform that role, but also mention they provide counseling and education. They assume without teaching abstinence that youth will be sexually active therefore they should be given ''protection.'' This logic parallels allowing me to watch television to secure information because I don't read because you didn't teach me.

I have thought about this issue long and hard and while I acknowledge that many youth are going to be sexually active because of the present media that our children are indoctrinated with each and every day, we cannot presume that youth would completely ignore a sex education program that would include values, prayer, reverence for God, and the acknowledgement that sex and marriage needs to be intertwined. We have nothing to lose and everything to gain. If for no other reason, we simply have not tried what we used to do historically. It is obvious that the present program of distributing protection has not reduced unwanted pregnancies or sexually transmitted diseases.

The next area that I want to look at is marriage versus just "living together." Throughout the months that I was writing this book, one of the major questions that I was asking people nationwide was "What rationale would you use to convince someone who was living together or 'shacking' to marry?" Many people that I talked to had real difficulties answering this question which reflects how far we have gone. We have strayed away from traditional African and American values. Many of the supporters of shacking advocate that they have the same quality relationship as people that are married. They are able to eschew the expense of a wedding. They are able to avoid the legal expenses of divorce and the bitterness that often accrue from the settlement of property.

Many people have commented that when they lived together for five and six years, it was a beautiful relationship and as soon as they got married the relationship took a downhill turn. I remember one comment that I received where they mentioned that when they had children the woman had her name legally changed to his so that everyone in the household had the same last name, yet, they still had not married! An additional remark that I heard is that another couple went as far as developing a legal contract so that in case one of the parties died, there was a legal design on how assets would be distributed. Yet they still chose not to marry. I would like to pause now and ask you if you were talking to someone, including yourself, what would be your best argument for why someone should marry versus shacking. Traditionally, marriage has been understood as a ''social obligation'' - an institution designed mainly for economic security and child rearing. The proportion of one adult's life spent with spouse and children was 62% in 1960 - the highest in our history. Today it has dropped to 43% - the lowest.[3] Today marriage is understood mainly to be a path toward self-fulfillment. People talk today about their emotional, sexual, material, intellectual needs, and the need to assert themselves. When people discuss these unfulfilled potentials and the need to keep growing they seem to take these metaphors literally - almost as if they believe the process of filling their unmet needs. It's like filling a set of wine glasses at a dinner party: the more needs filled the greater the self-fulfillment.

Psychological expectations for marriage become even higher - expectations fueled our society's high divorce rate. Divorce also feeds upon itself. The more divorce there is the more normal it becomes. The fewer negative sanctions there are to oppose it and the more potential new partners there are further compounds the dilemma. It used to be that if a person found out that you were married then they understood you were off limits, but now the popular phrase is ''Are you happily married?'' As long as you are not happily married then ''we can deal.'' This is all a reflection of the change in our values from God, MAAT and the Nguzo Saba to Hip-Hop and New Jack.

By now you should have been able to think about the rationale you would use to explain to someone why they should marry versus living together and shacking. These are some of the major reasons that I offer to people that are still perplexed about which way they should go. My first response is because God said so - because it's in his word, 2) marriage shows a greater commitment to the relationship. The commitment is not only confessed to you, individually, it is also confessed to God, to the church, and to all the family and friends that were in attendance at the ceremony, 3) it provides an example for the children so that when they become adults they will also know how to relate to each other, and 4) it provides stability. It shows a long-term commitment to the relationship.

Over the years, what I've attempted to do is to not only understand my value system, but also to try to understand the values of others. In listening to the major arguments for why people propose to shack versus marry, what I hear in the logic is that because the values of America have become so warped, where the institution of marriage is taken very lightly, where if all my needs are not fulfilled, then I can simply leave you and find someone else. It is understandable why people that operate from that value system choose to shack. They really are not convinced that the marriage should last a lifetime. There would be no need to shack, to try it out, to see how it works, let's practice for five years, if they were convinced that the institution of marriage was for a lifetime. The decision to shack is simply a rationale which is faulty because two wrongs do not make a right. The concept is because marriage is not working then let's try shacking.

The second analysis that I'd like to offer here is in terms of male responsibility. If males are not taught to be responsible in the smaller areas: cleaning up their rooms, completing their chores, keeping their notebook in order, managing their allowance, maintaining good grades, being punctual, then in the larger areas they will also be irresponsible. I have a theory that says

135

some mothers raise their daughters and love their sons. We have forty-year-old boys still living at home with their mothers. There are many males that spend their entire lives vacillating between the mother that they are able to live with and their girlfriend that allow him to shack. They simply never have to grow up and become responsible. Both women allow them to be irresponsible.

The dilemma that many women tell me they have with the male shortage is that when they talk to brothers about commitment and marriage the brothers either go away or say "I need more time." Even though we've now been living together for five years they still need "more time." Of course what should be obvious is that why should men make a further commitment when they can receive all the benefits of marriage without any additional responsibility.

The next major issue that has been greatly affected by values is abortion. Nationwide, you have seen marches and demonstrations that have erupted in violence as both pro-life and pro-choice advocates have voiced their opinions. One of the best ways to resolve an issue and to avoid complexities and factors that people bring to bear is to ask the fundamental question, "What does God have to say about abortion?" Then the answer becomes very clear that the Lord is pro-life. Being pro-life does not mean that there are not additional choices once that first decision has been made. A person can choose to bring the baby to term because it is part of their value system and it is consistent with their relationship to God. That person can then give the child up for adoption. These two words look so similar and yet we hear so much about the former and very little about the latter. We need to hear more about adoption and remove some of the anxiety, tension, emotion, and volatility from the issue. Senator Carol

Moseley-Braun gave one of the best answers during her campaign when she said that she is pro-life as an individual, but she is pro-choice as it relates to the government because she did not feel the government should be involved in this issue. This is an individual issue that has to be decided between the woman and the Lord. The government should not be involved in that equation. While I believe Carol felt that way, I also thought it was a very calculated political move that was made because theoretically, it is correct that the government should not be involved in this issue. The reality is that if the government does not provide funds for low income women that choose an abortion in effect what has happened is that abortion then becomes only an option for those financially able. Poor women, specifically women of color, will then utilize the butchers in the alleys. Overall, white women have 274 reported abortions per every thousand babies they actually bear. For black women the ratio is 635 per thousand, or 2.3 times the figure for whites. Among unmarried women - who account for about 80% of all abortions - white women are twice as likely to terminate a pregnancy. More black single women want their babies after marriage, however black women are almost three times as likely to seek abortion. The main reason is that black married couples are less regular users of birth control."[4] I believe it is a contradiction for the Republican Party and ''conservative democrats'' to be pro-life on the front end and pro-death on the back end. There is a contradiction for politicians to advocate life and then not properly fund Headstart, Chapter I, Pell Grants, and employment opportunities while allocating 1/3 of the budget to the military. Unless the objective is to be pro-life and then send all these underfunded children to the military and place

137

them on the front line. One progressive politician commented by asking everyone in the House and the Senate to raise their hands if they had any relatives on the front line in the Persian Gulf. As you can imagine no one raised their hand. The next major issue that we need to look at as it relates to values is welfare. I indicated earlier that America has no intention of balancing the budget and providing government cost effective programs. That's not in their repertoire of values. The country is willing to give someone $500 in a combination of AFDC and food stamps times 12 months for $6,000 not to work. If multiplied by 40 years this totals $240,000. I have said in many public speeches that if I was president I would end welfare later that evening, but unlike the Republican Party, I would replace it with each individual receiving $40,000 in scholarship monies for college and upon graduation $60,000 either to start their own business or to purchase a house. Of course all this money will be monitored to make sure that it's used for those purposes. That totals $100,000. As you can see the government is willing to spend $240,000 for a program that makes people dependent when there are other programs that would empower people. It is a decision based on values.

There are numerous women that have told me that they do not want welfare. They wouldn't mind working at McDonald's or anywhere, but can the government at least allow them to keep their green card and provide child care? Of course, the government flatly refuses. It would be more cost effective to allow the welfare recipient to receive the green card for medical care and child care and remove the person from the public dole. There are too many instances where the larger American public has seen the unemployed, portrayed by the media as lazy, lined up around buildings at even the slightest "rumor" that there were jobs available. It is obvious that many of these recipients do not suffer from a lack of work ethic. If anything they suffer from a capitalistic system that operates on the value of the exploitation of labor. Their labor costs can be driven downward if you structure a labor reserve i.e., an unemployed population, and if you consistently look for other markets worldwide where you can secure labor for less than a dollar an hour.

The concern that everyone should have about the 35.5 million Americans who are living below the poverty line should not only be an indictment to the American economy but looking at this population in more detail you begin to understand the feminization of poverty. Thirty-eight percent of all single White women with children live below the poverty line and fifty percent of all single African American women with children live below the poverty line. In an economy where a male truck driver is paid $10-$18 an hour and a female clerical worker is paid between four and seven dollars an hour, you begin to understand the concept of the working poor. What makes this issue more complex is that on the one hand America seems to have problems with African American women receiving welfare and remaining at home with their children, while the reality shows there are more White women at home on welfare raising their children than African Americans. The contradiction that we need to also explore here is that theoretically America values women staying home and rearing their children, unless they are women of color who are at home not because of their husbands income but because of governmental assistance. Yet the contradiction becomes further exasperated when we find out that there are 300,000 White widows who have children who are at home with their children, but they are at home not because of welfare, but because their White husband died and left them with income from Social Security.[5] Then we have to raise the question, "Is it desirable for women to stay home and nurture and educate their children?" Is it okay to stay home if you are a White female living below the poverty line - but not African American? Is it okay to stay home as a White female widow if your source of income is Social Security and not AFDC? What criteria and value are we using to determine what is right and what is wrong?

The next issue is gun control as it relates to values. Most legislation is trying to monitor the sales of guns either in the form of delayed purchases or some degree of reduction of guns has been defeated because of a strong lobby by the NRA (National Riflemen Association) and also by the advocates of the Constitution that allows Americans to bear arms. Two values surface here. The first one is obvious and that's money. It has been said that you can buy politicians very cheaply and the NRA consistently has been able to do that. Secondly, America's desire to bear arms shows the correlation between that desire and what happened in South Central LA. America was founded on violence. Columbus did not discover America - he invaded America and from that time hence Americans have consistently taken more and more land from the Native Americans. For a country that was founded on violence and has in its constitution the desire to bear arms, it is consistent and understandable that the majority would be against gun control.

As an African American writer concerned about the plight of our community where each year cities are breaking records, where many cities have over a thousand homicides a year among African Americans and with African American males leading the country in terms of homicides, where one of every 21 African

American males will be killed by another African American male. The issue of gun control speaks directly to the issue of values because the issue unfortunately is not the gun. If people hate themselves then as we see in prison, it does not matter what is the object. It could be a knife, kitchen utensil, a scarf or a sock that they would use in strangulation.

Even though I would offer that while the desire to kill someone exists regardless of a gun there are some major benefits to the gun that Africans found out when Europeans invaded Africa with their guns. The major benefits of a gun of course are its speed, distance and effectiveness. It is more difficult having a drive-by murder if you have to use a knife, kitchen utensil or a sock. Distance would be a problem, effectiveness would be limited and speed would be curtailed. This has major implications with the kind of arsenal that has been exported to the Black community by the oppressor. Many conscious African Americans also point out that when the police department asks for all guns to be turned in voluntarily, the major concern is that will the members of the NRA, KKK and the other 300 White supremacy organizations in America comply?

If we're going to talk about gun control we need to also talk about the police department because there are other countries throughout the world where the police departments do not use guns. After the Rodney King beating, we know that not every police officer is emotionally fit to use a gun or any other weapon. Carl Bell, an M.D. in Psychiatry in Chicago also indicates that for residents to possess a gun thinking that it is going to be used against a burglar they need to be aware that the odds of using it against a burglar are remote in comparison to a spouse using it in anger against the other or the children unfortunately finding the weapon and using it against themselves. My value system based upon my relationship to God, MAAT and the Nguzo Saba dictates that my first value is pro-life and thou shalt not kill. Therefore, the first item is that we need to teach our population to respect life because the fundamental issue is not the weapon, but the person's values who possesses the weapon. This first point does not negate the second and that is as a responsible citizen we must reduce and eliminate the possibilities of homicide. For that reason, my values dictate that I am in favor of gun control.

The last issue that I want to look at as it relates to values is the decriminalization of drugs. I thought long and hard about whether I want to even discuss this issue in this book. It is a very volatile issue and it is a very good possibility that half of my readers are going to disagree over this issue. I think we must analyze the impact drugs are having on the values of our children. There are young people that have lost the desire to pursue an education and working hard because they believe there is more money to be earned selling drugs. The gang problem has escalated not because gangs are more popular in this present era than they were before, but due to the lack of jobs. Gangs are becoming the major distributor of drugs.

Criminal justice experts acknowledge that we do not have a gang problem. We have an economic problem which resembles the kinds of wars that exist with Coca Cola and Pepsi and any other competitor in a particular industry fighting over turf. Gangs see drugs as a very profitable item and they simply are protecting their market share. This is very different from gangs of yesteryear that simply disagreed about the color of their hats, and which side of the tracks they resided. This is now an economic battle over the distribution of drugs. Sixty percent of all inmates that are presently in jail are there because of drug related crimes. Seventy percent of all property crimes are also related to drugs. Approximately, 75% of all murders in the African American community are related to drugs.[6] America could not build prisons fast enough to address the drug problem and yet there is an attempt to do that with over half of the drug budget being allocated to prisons versus more cost effective allocations. Maybe politicians are not aware that you can maintain access to drugs while incarcerated.

The fundamental problem should be obvious. There is a values crisis in America. People have a void and want to feel good. A people with a spiritual void who are not anchored in God, who do not have a value system based on MAAT and the Nguzo Saba will look to external sources for the next high. What makes this issue very complex is that we have been here before. In the late 1920s, America faced the same dilemma as it related to the legalization of alcohol. America made the decision to legalize alcohol because their population expressed a tremendous desire to drink. Crime was escalating then as now fueled by drugs. Remember, alcohol is a drug. As I pointed out in Chapter Two on the power of the media, 6,000 Americans died last year from hard drugs, 100,000 died of alcohol and 434,000 died from lung cancer as a result of nicotine.

Can you imagine the legalization of drugs and Americans not only being able to go to a store and secure a bottle of Old English 800 but also several packs of heroin, crack and cocaine? Can you imagine driving down the street where there's a driver coming towards you who is totally strung out on crack? Can you imagine your bus driver, airplane pilot, and doctor and any other professional performing their duty for your benefit while under the influence of these harder drugs? For that reason I understand why numerous politicians have disagreed with Mayor Kurt Schmoke in Baltimore who recommended either the legalization or decriminalization of drugs, or at least to look at this issue as a medical and health problem. This policy presently exists in England, where they have reduced crime, incarceration rates and new offenders. The critics of legalization need to acknowledge the this present drug policy is not working. This parallels the issue of should we marry or should we shack, because two wrongs do not make a right. I am very much aware that if my value system is pro-life, pro-God, pro-MAAT and the Nguzo Saba that it will be inconsistent for me to recommend the legalization, decriminalizing, or viewing drugs as a health problem with the rationale being that people are going to consume it anyway. Please appreciate this is not my first desire. The first desire would be a stronger educational program based on values with the foundation being in God to remove our desire for drugs. Just as our sex education program lacks these religious principles our drug education program does also. Secondly, more monies need to be allocated on protecting our borders and preventing drugs from entering. Third, the drug industry is valued at a hundred and fifty billion dollars and we have to believe that the banks are involved in laundering the money. Therefore, an effective program would monitor the banks. Fourth, many of us do not realize that 76% of all drug users are White and yet 60% of the prosecutions are African Americans. That is discrimination, racism, and an expression of people's values.

To effectively deal with the drug problem we need to be more aggressive about incarcerating the White drug users. African Americans primarily are drug dealers because of the shortage of jobs that are available to them. A stronger economic program would reduce African Americans from selling drugs. African Americans are becoming aware that the average drug dealer does not make $2,000 a day, but according to three independent studies makes $700.00 a month.[7] If we don't want to consider decriminalizing drugs we need to view it as a health problem. Drug users, in many cases, want to be arrested because they have found out that the only way for them to receive medical service is through the prisons. More monies need to be allocated for treatment centers. All of these issues pertaining to drugs goes back to our values and the criteria we would use to make a decision. My major concern on this issue is that African Americans have been able to withstand the middle passage, slavery and the depression, but this issue of drugs has now become so intense that if African American leaders and/or the government do not make decisions soon that are in our best interest then we have a Hip-Hop, New Jack generation that may very well self-destruct.

In conclusion, we have attempted throughout this book to see if we can upgrade our value system from Hip-Hop and New Jack to MAAT and the Nguzo Saba. I never will forget giving a workshop at the Black United Front Conference where Chokwe Lumumba heard me speak. He said it was an excellent workshop, especially if the objective is to stay in America. However, he told me afterwards, that he was seriously questioning whether an African can prosper in America. When the statistics near 40% and 50% in every major facet affecting life, then it becomes obvious that the problem has exceeded the individual - it's something about America's values and it's racist structure. That makes it very difficult for Africans to practice the virtue of MAAT and the Nguzo Saba. The advertising budget for all products hovers around 30 billion dollars. Compare that to the ad budget promoting positive values that are God centered to reinforce righteousness, harmony, truth, justice, balance, reciprocity, and order. We need values and advertisements which will promote unity, self-determination, collective work and responsibility, cooperative economics, purpose, creativity, and faith. When you compare the Western budget that promotes New Jack and Hip-Hop to the Eastern budget that promotes God, MAAT, and the Nguzo Saba it is obvious why we are in trouble. That's what has made this book very frustrating because the few ads that promote these values and the few books that talk about the challenge are minuscule in comparison to this 30 billion dollar budget that has calculated that in 30 seconds they can influence the viewing public to buy whatever they want. The scope or extent of this pervasive and insidious value system has caused a sense of frustration to many but solutions are available.

Gail Inlow points out that "Most adapt the values from the culture. A few develop a new set - they are the prime movers of progress." Scripture reminds us that the harvest is large and the workers are few. Wide is the gate to hell and narrow is the entrance into eternity. We must be the few. We must be the example of the value system that taught our people long ago. We are not a new people. Life began in Africa. The values of cooperation, harmony and righteousness began in Africa. We must be the few that save the Hip-Hop and New Jack generation. We cannot save them with arrogance and a blacker-than-thou attitude. We must save them as Jesus saved the Samaritan woman at the well by going out to where she was, showing compassion and meeting her at her point of need and empowering her. God Bless!

REFERENCES

Introduction
1) "Reaching the Hip-Hop Generation," MEE Productions, Philadelphia, 1992, pp. vii, 1,3,27.

2) Maulana Karenga, *"Toward a Sociology of Maatian Ethics: Literature and Context,"* Egypt Revisited, Edited, Ivan Van Sertima, (New Brunswick: Transaction 1989) pp. 373, 383.

Chapter Two
1) Michael Pfleger, Press Release July 15, 1992 on billboard saturation by Gateway.

2) Smokefree Educational Services, Inc., New York, NY.

3) Chicago Lung Association, "Booze and Butts Billboards in Fifty Chicago Neighborhoods: Market Segmentation to Promote Dangerous Products to the Poor." 1990

4) *Chicago Tribune*, "Snuff Out Camel Ads, Doctors Ask," March 10, 1992, Section I, p. 3.

5) Laurie Abraham, "City Balks as Billboards Overrun Poor Areas," *Chicago Reporter*, Vol. 19, No. 10, Nov. 1990.

6) Center for Science in the Public Interest, "Malt Liquor - Alcohol Content, August 1989.

7)   Marin Institute for Prevention of Alcohol and Other Drug Problems, "Malt Liquor Fact Sheet.," M. Shanken, "The U.S. Beer Market," *Impact Data Review and Forecast,* 1990 Edition.

8)   George Hacker, Ronald Collins, and Michael Jacobson, *Marketing Booze to Blacks* (Washington: Center for Science in the Public Interest, 1987), pp. 9-10

9)   "Reaching the Hip-Hop Generation," MEE Productions, Philadelphia, 1992, pp. 57,75,84.

10) Kenneth Clark, "Yes, TV Violence is Awful, But What's the Cure?" *Chicago Tribune,* Oct. 25, 1992, Section 4, p. 1.

11) *Black Issues in Higher Education,* Oct. 8, 1992, p. 23.

12) Lynette Freidrich Cofer, "The Emotional Core of Family Concerns," *Family Affairs,* Institute for American Values, Vol. 3, No. 1-2, Spring - Summer 1990 p. 7.

13) "Reaching the Hip-Hop Generation," op. cit pp. 63-65.

Chapter Three
1)   Johari Kunjufu, "Behavior and It's Value Base," *Black Books Bulletin,* Vol. 4, No. 3, Fall 1976, pp. 40-43.

2)   Julius Nyerere, *Ujamaa: Essays on Socialism,* (Dar es Salaam: Oxford University Press, 1968) pp. 2,7.

3) William Griggs, *The Megalite Connection,* (Chicago: E & L Press, 1990) p. 131.

4) Masaru Ibuka, *Kindergarten is Too Late,* (New York: Simon & Schuster, 1977) p. 24.

5) Jawanza Kunjufu, *To Be Popular or Smart: The Black Peer Group,* (Chicago: African American Images, 1988) p. 52.

6) Robert Merton, *Social Theory and Social Structure,* (New York: Mac Millan, 1968) pp. 193-211.

7) Leon Bing, *Do or Die,* (New York: Harper Collins 1991) p. 221.

8) Samuel Proctor, *My Moral Odyssey,* (Valley Forge: Judson Press, 1989) p. 54.

9) William Cross Jr, *Shades of Black,* (Philadelphia: Temple University Press, 1991) pp. 191-223.

10) Bing, op. cit, pp. 120-127.

11) Wade Nobles, *African Psychology,* (Oakland: Black Family Institute 1986) p. 21.

12) Linda James Myers, *Understanding an Afrocentric World View,* (Dubuque: Kendall Hunt, 1988) pp. 91-92.

13) Paul Hill Jr., *Coming of Age: African American Male Rites of Passage,* (Chicago: African American Images, 1992) pp. 66-67, 75-76.

14) Yosef ben Jochannan, *African Origins of the Major Western Religions,* (New York: Alkebu-Lan Books, 1970) pp. 69-70

15) David Barton, *America: To Pray or Not To Pray,* (Aledo, TX: Wall Builder Press, 1991) pp. 11, 30, 35, 41, 47, 55, 87.

16) WYCA Christian Radio Broadcast, April, 1992.

17) Maulana Karenga, *Selections from The Husia,* (Los Angeles: University of Sankore Press, 1984) pp. 17, 41-43, 93.

Chapter Four
1) Manning Marable, *Race Reform and Rebellion,* (Jackson, MS: University Press of Mississippi, 1991) p. 187.

2) *U.S. Statistical Abstracts 1990.*

3) William Julius Wilson, *The Truly Disadvantaged,* (Chicago: University of Chicago Press, 1987) p. 13.

4) ibid., pp. 73-74

5) Andrew Hacker, *Two Nations,* (New York: Charles Scribner, 1992) p. 4.

6) Interview with Peter Brown, author of *Minority Party,* on ''Tony Brown's Journal,'' November 22,1991.

7) Hacker, op. cit, p. 36.

8) Jonathan Kozol, *Savage Inequalities,* (New York: Crown Publishers, 1991) pp. 236-237.

9) Gail Inlow, *Values in Transition,* (New York: Wiley, 1972) p. 45.

10) John Perkins, *With Justice For All,* (Ventura, CA: Regal Books 1982) pp. 52-55.

Conclusion

1) Barton, op. cit., p. 36.

2) David Popenoe, "The Family Transformed," *Family Affairs,* The Institute for American Values, Vol. 2, No. 2-3 Summer/Fall 1989, pp. 1-2.

3) Ibid., p.2.

4) Hacker, op. cit., pp. 80-81.

5) ibid, pp. 91-92.

6) Oliver Johnson, *Breaking the Chains of Cocaine: Black Male Addiction and Recovery,* (Chicago: African American Images, 1992) p. 25.

7) Earl Ofari Hutchinson, *The Mugging of Black America,* (Chicago:African American Images, 1990) p. 54.